From left to right:
Sandra (daughter) Alice (granddaughter) Barbara (wife)
At the Trafford Centre 2019

BELIEF

Lifetime Recollections

BELIEF

Lifetime Recollections

Colin Potts, QPM

ARTHUR H. STOCKWELL LTD
Torrs Park, Ilfracombe, Devon, EX34 8BA
Established 1898
www.ahstockwell.co.uk

British Library Cataloguing-in-Publication Data.
A catalogue record for this book is available
from the British Library.

ISBN 978-0-7223-5037-9
Printed in Great Britain by
Arthur H. Stockwell Ltd
Torrs Park   Ilfracombe
Devon EX34 8BA

CONTENTS

at Bowerfold; Time Expired; Where's the Body?; Indomitable Spirits in the Slums; Barbara Gives Birth to Sandra; 'It's a Long Way to Tipperary' (Jack Judge); Rod Laver v Ken Rosewall; Mistaken Identity?; Fighting at the Bus Station; *Streets away from Paradise*, by Eli Hague; Sandra Goes Paddling.

Wall; Trouble on the Home Watch Bus; Councillor Glynn Evans; Initial Effects and Police Hostilities; Impersonating a Police Officer; Park Watch, Fairywell; Probation Service; Man Down; A Ten-Year-Old Boy in the Cells; A Casual Visitor; The Home Secretary Visits; 'Inspector Jigsaw'; Salford University.

INTRODUCTION

The majority of people who write an account of their life story appear to be a mixture of recognisable celebrities, those who have achieved some form of notoriety that some people would find interesting or those who have excelled in a walk of life that they have been engaged in. I can't lay claim to any of those, but what they all have in common is that no two life stories are the same.

I wrote my life story by accident. During my final week before retiring as the security manager at a large NHS trust my colleagues were anxious for me to give them time to chat over some of the interesting issues I had dealt with throughout my career. I had worked as their security manager for eighteen years, and they were vaguely aware of some of my previous job experiences. They were also intrigued about incidents that had come my way, and they were keen to grill me about my policing career as they suspected there were some juicy bits lurking in the shadows which by my nature I had never brought to light. They were all bound together by a belief that I had augmented many changes for the better at their hospital and they didn't want to miss their last opportunity to gain the truth about incidents they had only gained information about through the 'grapevine'. They made their way in groups of two or three to my office, made themselves comfortable and eagerly waited for me to skip through my life story. Or was it the tea and biscuits? As it happened, it didn't really matter as they were consumed by their own silence and listened intently. Whilst it was uncharted territory, I quickly recognised that they started to exude the youthful innocence and wonderment I first encountered when I told bedtime stories to my daughter and granddaughter. For those who have never had to undertake this task I would implore you to seize any opportunity offered which effectively allows you to hold your audience in some kind of spellbound trance with the result being delivered the following night when your presence becomes a necessity; not to be available for another rendition is not recommended if you want to maintain domestic harmony. At that point I felt stirrings of interest in committing my exploits to a more permanent record. Nevertheless the above reasons wouldn't sustain my interest to reach into the past, but the pendulum to feed inspiration lay closer to home insofar that I realised ancestry information within our family was extremely sparse with my daughter and family settling in France and two of my three sisters settling with their families in Canada. The scene was firmly set; all that was necessary was to devote time and effort. That was the easy bit.

I always felt that of the six children in our family I was the least communicative, often dismissing interest in myself by informing others that I am just an old plod who just happens to have won life's lottery. That conceals the real me. My life has had many twists and turns, some death-defying, some with experiences that belong in another world that I still don't understand, some commenting about the human feelings of police officers in times of stress and their humour, including some inspirational moments and some extremely gut-wrenching and very sad incidents.

Against this background and intertwined with these experiences, my upbringing during my early years is coloured by the Second World War, food rationing (including other essential life-supporting items) and the discipline required within a family of three sisters and two brothers. This family and community social experience is now largely lost in time, but in recalling some facts they give colour to a most austere black-and-white existence, which was endured by many. The effects of our early domestic existence seemed to predetermine our journeys along our separate paths – and for me particularly as my journey arose out of abject poverty, sacrifice, persistence and unpredictable situations which brought out some great human qualities that I wouldn't fully appreciate until later in life. Other very important influences that crashed into my life were often in the form of inspirational people from the most improbable sources. Their wisdom, advice, patience, humour and belief often in unlikely situations were again only appreciated by me much later in life.

But my story isn't unique. It may at times stretch the imagination, but I believe that in the twenty-first century there are legions of people who are in situations which allow greater flexibility over their time, and many will have tremendously worthy stories that their families and maybe the book-reading section of our society would find interesting and absorbing. To them my simple message is find a pen or let your fingers run riot across the typewriter keys. I have made every effort to avoid making any political comment, and where villains appear in recent times I haven't revealed their identities. This didn't blunt my energy to discover that spark of belief in others and create what influence you are able to give. It could be that there are parents who are unsung heroes and will forever remain so although they are an ever present shining example to their family – such as my mother, Alice. You could be struggling at school or doing a 'nothing' job or not able to get employed or feel you have lost your way, or suffocating because a loss of direction or guidance has culminated in a loss of will or the courage to take a new direction in life. Everyone has the ability to influence others, and sometimes this is all it takes to make a difference. Believe you can do it and you have already made that all-important start. But this belief has a double edge. It is that which others invest in you and conversely what you can invest in others. My story also reveals that this help manifests itself in the most unusual circumstances. Blink and that moment may be lost. Lose concentration at your peril. There is no substitute for staying alert, so take advantage of those glimmers of inspiration and be aware they may come from the most unlikely sources. Your contribution, no matter how insignificant it may seem to you, could be that small yet significant life changer to others.

To this end change is often driven by criticism, and my opinions attempt to reveal shortcomings with constructive comments to feed change in an endeavour to foster improvements. My story begins as basically a simple story about country folk. As it progresses it gives me the opportunity to remind us of changes in life that are seeping into our social fabric, creating social disconnects about which we are largely aware – though we may be unaware of the lasting effects of this creeping disease. My theme of keeping things simple as a key to success is supported by my actions to acknowledge the value of face-to-face social interactions and the often unrecognised importance of location, which I refer to and demonstrate as the positive transformative effect of proximity.

My story could have been set in the 1830s as often depicted in the novels of Catherine Cookson because our domestic scene seemed to be trapped in that era, but I begin 100 years later. My mother and father were living in a small two-up-and-two-down cottage in the countryside near Middlewich in mid Cheshire. My two brothers and two sisters (sister Ellen Anne was to arrive in 1947) ensured that the house was in continuous chaos, but this was our normal. I was the fourth child. Dad was a farm labourer and my mother kept her brood well fed, though mainly on very basic food, and dressed in clothes that today would be refused by some of our high-street charity shops. Our existence was influenced by the Second World War and the breadline level of income labouring classes were struggling with.

In this family circle my mother's words were not to be disobeyed; she managed to keep us generally out of trouble and maintained family discipline. She was always in charge, and she had a physical presence of authority, usually wrapped in an apron with her hair kept in check by a turban. She had to make some difficult decisions, yet somehow she managed to retain that caring love of a mother hen. The Second World War was starting to impact on our lives. We all thought it exciting, but that wouldn't last. Dad died suddenly in 1941. Without any income to sustain the family, my mother took some drastic actions to keep her family together. Whilst we all struggled to live with her actions, we ultimately accepted that she didn't have any alternative. Her own personal sacrifice must have been enormous, but her indomitable spirit didn't include quitting; and against what we may come to see to be overwhelming odds she carried on. Living in dire poverty, not realising where the next slice of bread was coming from, huddling around the open fire created close family bonds. Each protected the others. Everything was shared equally and family games were totally inclusive.

We existed within a small hamlet where all neighbours made it their business to know each other and everyone was held in mutual respect even though we were a bunch of unkempt and unruly children. It was this unseen bond of neighbourliness that would much later stir again as I struggled to recreate this village concept as an answer to lawlessness and rampant crime. This was an important aspect of our upbringing, where we blissfully survived in our little world – and we were happy.

My schooldays and achievements in lessons were at best average, but this started to change due the belief of a particular senior teacher and the influence of a most unlikely person in unlikely circumstances: our milkman.

On leaving school my first boss was a local farmer. Often the work was physically hard, mind-bogglingly boring, often carried out in extreme weather or other conditions that were uncomfortable and exacerbated by my poor clothing. In reality these challenges will always appear at different times of life. They are a necessity if you are to nourish a belief in yourself and others around you. At that time my boss and other work colleagues were not just supportive, but inspirational. It was not what you might expect from a bunch of farm-labouring yokels. What they may have lacked in any academic prowess was compensated for by their basic human traits of sincerity, understanding and patience, and their mountain-high country and animal-husbandry skills. Humour and camaraderie were never far from the surface – traits which I often came to rely on later in my story. They may have looked uninspiring, but they were the product of hard times which had imbued common sense throughout their souls, because often their families' well-being relied upon them. My first boss was inspirational, immensely courageous and brave. One of my work colleagues roped me into going with other mates to be taught ballroom dancing. I relate the details of this later, not because one minute I was wearing jeans and clogs, the next sporting patent-leather shoes and tripping the light fantastic to artists such as Al Martino and Alma Cogan, but to capture the moment when I entered the big wide world and to explain an incident some sixteen years later at an indoor tennis tournament in Stalybridge, where I was mistaken for another person. But I was the one mistaken.

My police career made a hesitant start and my reminiscences of Hazel Grove and Stalybridge are through the eyes of a young inexperienced constable. My initial interview with the Chief Constable left me feeling he had lost the plot. His parting advice was that I should never forget his force only policed by public consent. For my ignorance I spent the next thirty-five years continually reminding myself that he hadn't lost the plot and I was the one who had much to learn. My first twelve months were to question my faith in the merits of policing and my suitability to do the job. Dealing with a fatal road accident involving a schoolboy forced me to walk down the world's longest driveway, and grappling successfully with a runaway horse careering out of control towards schoolchildren crossing the busy A6 was tempered with my all-important meeting with my future wife. At that point if there had been a national lottery then I had just scooped the first prize. I give insights into management styles, which as a young constable is another issue you need to persevere with. The impact of these experiences stayed imprinted in my memory only to later surface and make significant differences, together with the wisdom, advice and guidance of my first boss, which continued to influence my character and outlook. Nevertheless I was completely unprepared and have no explanation for two incidents that I quickly put to the back of my mind. The first was a near collision with a craft that I simply describe as resembling a flying saucer and the second was my witnessing some form of other dimension as I stopped to chat to a fellow police officer, which had fatal consequences. It seems so far-fetched that it simply couldn't be made up.

Policing in Manchester during the seventies and eighties continued my culture shocks, and I mention a couple of humorous incidents that arose from serious policing operations, the good and bad in policing management styles, the unseen, unreported human stories that should bring home the serious side of policing. Some of these will be brought to light during my account of the Woolworth's fire tragedy, including the emotional impact on officers and the quick-thinking fire officer who saved me from serious injury. At this point you would be forgiven for thinking that enough is enough for one life, but life doesn't happen that way.

The theme of 'Who watches the watchers?' had some dramatic twists. I was in charge of the city's undercover squad when it was discovered that our phone lines had been bugged. Immediately prior to this, I had conducted a clandestine meeting outside the walls of Strangeways Prison with a national-newspaper reporter masquerading as an informant who mistakenly thought he was talking in confidence to me as we sat together in my saloon car. Later, and in a totally separate incident, I was obliged to orchestrate the demise of two senior officers who thought they were a law unto themselves only to have their world crashing in around them. Other jaw-dropping incidents are revealed and you may consider what benevolent soul was passing on the information to bring these criminals to book. I don't know, but you should be mindful of my earlier role which propelled me into the spotlight of the city's 'mafia', who quite easily kept tabs on my policing activities as my appearance (red hair) resembled an angler's fishing float as it bobbed about on the water's surface. A previously undetectable case of porn trafficking was ironically unravelled due to information passed by those who were watching the watchers. I do suggest who the possible informants could have been. In another case, which ironically turned out to be a case of mistaken identity, personal life-threatening events were assuaged by my sergeant's swift intervention to effect an arrest. The reaction of the culprit at the conclusion of the court case was most surprising.

I served in Wythenshawe from 1987 to 1997. It was a most

rewarding experience. There I found residents, their families and businesses, including schools and their councillors, eager to create close bonds with their police, and in this book I reveal the unusual way in which we brought this into reality and why. They gave their time unstintingly and without question. Business leaders and councillors went the extra mile to help, and they succeeded. This was truly magnificent when compared with my first week at Wythenshawe, when two head teachers were clearly emotionally moved about their concerns for the well-being of their schools during the summer holidays, another head teacher flatly refused to interact with disaffected pupils and a Scout leader was reduced to tears and physical wreck as he described constant damage and vandal attacks on his Scout and Guide building, including physical attacks on his Scouts and Guides. Later we were to meet again before a Crown Court judge in a case in which the Scoutmaster successfully fought off allegations of improper conduct that caused him great pain and personal cost to his health and well-being.

The lack of police visually patrolling and creating their presence in the community had allowed other undesirable types to fill the void and the effects had silently crept up on the constabulary, and no more so than in Wythenshawe. A police colleague encouraged me to turn to Salford University for help. This resulted in three years of utilising my spare time grappling with what could have been a foreign language, but they called it 'marketing'. It was unbelievably helpful in designing our policing strategies in Wythenshawe. Even so, our first attempts to restore this delicate balance was met with local gangs launching vicious attacks with volleys of rocks aimed at the police together with these villains ambushing residents as they walked to our mobile outdoor community unit with threats as some kind of welcoming ritual to anyone who dared to challenge their control of the streets and communities in the suburbs of Manchester. They failed to reckon with the resolve of Wythenshawe people as these hostile actions only served to bind them together and deepen their cooperation with the police and community leaders. The vibrancy of this partnership would not be denied.

I describe many (but not all) of the actions we took, including the role of my sergeant, who led the front line and gave everything to the cause with his own brand of influence, belief and mutual trust in all those around him. He was my top sergeant and foot soldier, battling daily to recreate the 'village effect' and 'parish policing' across this vast housing estate, and for a decade he was immensely successful in managing his team, who effectively became the forerunners of the national Police & Community Support Officers Scheme. In a nutshell we did two things. Firstly we kept everything simple and secondly we delivered proactive policing with some examples that may surprise you. There were a couple occasions in the sixties and seventies when I raised my concerns about the withdrawal of front-line policing, but our policing hierarchy at that time were not in listening mode and you may conclude that this is the root of many of our current problems. Nevertheless they would never have envisaged the impact on human relationships caused by lack of social contact driven by the technological and digital era. This theme returns me to the advice I received as I joined the police service: "We only police with the consent of the public." But our policing strategies throughout the latter part of the twentieth century have actively isolated communities, creating 'police suburban wastelands' as contact with the public has progressively ebbed away.

I conclude my account of my police career by describing my visit to Buckingham Palace and the honour of talking to HRH Prince Charles.

Wythenshawe and Withington Hospitals had been a thorn in my side throughout my ten years of policing at Wythenshawe. They were active crime hot spots – easy targets for criminals against ineffective resident security teams. The reality was that their car parks were lined with broken glass as local criminals had a field day filling their boots whilst vehicle owners were visiting sick people.

On my retirement from the police I took up a position as the security manager at these two hospitals and set about the conversion to reflect the example where Wythenshawe had become a highly desirable and relatively low-crime residential area. Local police, community police support officers, residents, staff and businesses weighed in with their support. Mountains had to be scaled and were. For example, an arsonist started five fires at Wythenshawe Hospital, endangering the lives of patients and staff, which led to my agreement with the chief executive to use the 'Al Capone' approach as the most appropriate way to bring the matter to a successful conclusion. This leap of faith, was, however, overtaken by events which quickly secured a successful conclusion. It was the late nineties, but I was able to instigate actions of crime prevention and detection that were ground-breaking at that time.

The Scoutmaster mentioned earlier revealed his true feelings and that of so many of his colleagues and is an example of a belief which typifies that of so many residents of Wythenshawe and their personal sacrifices to develop a relatively crime-free town in which it is safe for people to go about their daily business, and the young people of Wythenshawe can fully develop their potential. I discovered theirs to be an outstanding example which is taking Wythenshawe forward into a positive future.

In my concluding chapter I briefly comment from the sidelines about policing and the National Health Service. I touch on some shortcomings, with the main intention of illustrating that throwing money at the problem will not in itself bring about desired conclusions and that challenging existing practices is often necessary if progress is to be made. Humans need to know they belong; the need for social contact is within us all and can fluctuate like personal appetites permeating like superglue, as we evidenced as we cultivated our parish policing initiative in Wythenshawe.

CHAPTER 1

No. 1 STANTHORNE CROSSROADS, MIDDLEWICH, CHESHIRE

My home town nestles on the Cheshire Plain and is enclosed by the Rivers Wheelock and Dane. The nature of these two rivers describes the course of my story. They meander gently as they sing their own song to the likes of herons, kingfishers, swallows and dragonflies, and they play host to a variety of small fish in a state of tranquillity that has persisted for many years but is destined to be short-lived as they are drawn to join larger rivers downstream. These slow and peaceful arteries of life twist and turn over shallow and deep sections in which predators and great dangers are concealed to the inexperienced eye, but to a young boy yet to go to school and oblivious to this rural beauty the rivers presented a scene of sheer excitement and wonderment as I tightly grasped my older sister's hand. These rivers could be seen as a reflection of my life's journey, but my world of innocence was a lifetime away from what life was to hold in store for me and my family. For now I gazed into the shallow sections, where the flow increased over rocks smoothed by the caressing actions of the water which chatted its gurgling sounds and in doing so gave a voice to the rivers.

The nature of these rivers had long since been exploited by previous generations as several watermills had provided essential economic support to the local population for the purpose of grinding locally grown corn (oats, wheat, barley) and beans between two large flat stones – as in the case of Rigby's Mill in Stanthorne, which we were to know it as during the forties – which utilised the power of the river as it turned the great wheels. Elsewhere wind which would catch the prevailing breezes to slowly and majestically and seemingly without effort move these great objects that would transfer their power to the large grinding stones. Local farmers would haul their corn by horse and cart and thereafter to the market for human consumption or as essential food for farm animals. It was a scene that was to fast disappear from the countryside as mechanisation, set to surge forward after the Second World War, would confirm.

The Kitchen Table, Burnt Toast and Five in a Bed

My mother and father moved into their dream cottage in the thirties. By 1939 they had five healthy children. Father was a farm labourer and his efforts to feed and clothe us all meant that he was always absent when the younger members were awake and creating mayhem. Our small cottage in the country had two bedrooms and two downstairs rooms. A temporary room on the ground floor leading directly off the living room had the only cold-water tap in the house with the only other notable feature being the large metal hook that was fixed into the ceiling. From this dead game and chickens were left hanging until prepared for the kitchen table. Our zinc bath and a dolly washing tub completed the kitchen furniture, which was continually in use. The living room had an open fireplace, and an easy chair on either side of the fire. A large square wooden table occupied a central position and a sofa was stood up against the wall opposite the fireplace. All family life was witnessed around this table. We all ate, played games, knitted scarves, darned gloves, sewed carpets from old rags and baked using the fireside oven. During the winter evenings our paraffin lamp, our sole source of lighting, took centre stage on this table. The lives of all our family unfolded around this table. It was our symbol of existence. Arguments and squabbles took place between brothers and sisters, but mainly family harmony persisted in a happy atmosphere with Mother as a bandleader figure who effortlessly held our attention and directed each one of us. Dissent would have required courage, and none of us yet possessed that quality.

Everyone had to learn the process of lighting the coal fire, which proved to be difficult if the sticks of wood were damp or the coal was wet. The difficult part was to then use a sheet of newspaper placed up against the fire to create additional draught. Often great excitement would break out when this newspaper caught fire. It was quickly stuffed up the chimney to prevent the house from being burnt to the ground, but that usually started a fire in the chimney as soot from previous fires blazed away, eventually exhausting its supply and tamely extinguishing itself. How we managed to avoid burning the house to the ground is a mystery.

Similarly, baking was a communal affair. But the reward we all had was to sample our efforts. Mother's speciality was to bake potato cakes from the dinner leftovers and the fat from whatever meat dish was roasted in the fireside oven. The oven cooked them to perfection and each potato cake, the size of a saucer, was sliced horizontally, and either buttered or spread with black treacle. Once you had served and passed the eating apprenticeship you devoured with ease and relish, but essentially the skill was to avoid allowing any excess butter or treacle to run on to your hands and arms. There was never anything left as the table would proudly display clean plates and contented children.

Similar to the potato cake, food at mealtimes may have been basic, but it was where we were taught and given life's essential tools, and it was where we created and cemented close bonds between brothers and sisters. However, probably the most important skill we all had to master was to convert a slice of bread into that appealing brown appetising slice of toast and at times share it. Everyone had to take charge of the toasting job in the morning. To my brothers and sisters the fire-blackened two-pronged two-foot-long metal toasting fork was the most important kitchen utensil we had. It lived permanently on the hearth at the side of the fire. Everyone devoured their portions. Everyone had burnt fingers and newly designed heat-influenced eyebrows – the process usually left us with one singed eyebrow and therefore my sisters quickly became world experts at inventing successful avoidance techniques. We spread the toast with butter, dripping fat, black treacle or home-made jam. We could have had a feast, but our supply of bread was extremely limited as everything seemed to be rationed or we didn't have the money to purchase it. As this breakfast ritual gathered speed, a toasted-bread smell would be announced to the half a dozen nearby houses, with our ravenous appetites only giving way to collective shouts of alarm if the unfortunate one in charge of the toasting fork had hovered too long over the fire's hot coals with a telltale plume of burnt bread adding to their embarrassment and ridicule. Often the sound of our approaching school bus would supersede breakfast arrangements as everyone had to be ready and waiting at the bus stop, which was directly outside the house. These sudden exoduses, like rats fleeing a sinking ship, would in a stroke, whilst leaving the kitchen with pots all around the table, restore some kind of tranquillity that would remain until we invaded again later in the day.

We all slept in one double bed. In the harsh cold winters this was definitely beneficial as any other source of heat was non-existent. I was by far and away the most disruptive and argumentative of all the children, which was confirmed by my mop of red hair. Both myself and my immediately elder sister shared this trait with the addition of body-covering freckles. My two brothers and eldest sister were not similarly blessed or handicapped as they had dark-brown hair.

Our only toilet was at the far end of the yard. It was emptied once a week by our local council. If they failed due to weather conditions (which wasn't often) Mother and I would struggle to carry a large metal toilet dish into our rear garden and empty it into a hole we had previously dug. We hated this task, but it had to be done.

We were all very young and during the early forties many others were in the same boat. Poverty crashed into our faces at almost every turn, but the irony was that our close family structure ensured that we were not poor. We always had our family conversations and housework to do to keep us busy, and neighbours were kind and always had time to greet us and talk to us. The effect of having good neighbours living in the dozen and a half houses around this crossroads would remain with me and much later form the strategy to restore a semblance of this village existence on one of Europe's largest housing estates, which had gained the reputation of being a high-crime area ruled by criminal gangs. Some of the neighbours were what we would now regard as being middle-class, but you would never have guessed. A neighbour was an extension of our family and I was to witness this first-hand and sooner than I would have wished.

On reflection, we were a happy lot, living in the country, equal members of the community, a strong village resonance in our daily lives. Although we were existing from day to day, often hand to mouth, all these neighbours would always acknowledge our presence and show genuine interest in our welfare. This was prior to the creation of the NHS. Knowing that any of these neighbours would help must have given Mother that inner warm glow of belonging and being a respected partner in that small village setting. All five of us children were outrageously healthy, but it wasn't to last.

Dad Dies, 1941

My youngest brother and I could never recall anything about our father as he died in 1941. Living and surviving had just become more difficult. Just how Mother managed or even coped with this body blow could never be fully appreciated by any of her children. Looming on the horizon was the threat of an enemy invasion, but nearer to home this proud imposing figure almost always dressed in a full-length pinafore and a turban around her head was setting out to do battle against any well-meaning attempts to separate her children and cocoon them away in some distant children's home. To remove any of her children would have literally been over her dead body. It didn't happen.

Elder Brother Les Leaves the Family Home

Mother decided that she would send her eldest son to live with her mother, about four miles away. At this time I was one of five children at home. This event brought about a significant change in our lives. It affected all of our family, but my brother and two sisters probably had little appreciation of the trauma that Leslie (Les) would have to experience. He had lost his brothers and sisters and the family life in our close-knit family. It would have been a new start for him, but he never complained. In effect his visits to the family home became more infrequent. He had to attend a different school, create new friends in a strange town and live in a house with no other children. He had drawn the short straw. We enjoyed his infrequent visits to us and we would all look forward with much excitement to when he came to visit us.

Grandma volunteered to look after a young boy for a couple of years. He was a similar age to Les and because of the war had been moved out of Liverpool. To us country children he spoke a foreign language. It wasn't, but we had great difficulties understanding his accent. We did, however, share the same passion for football. Les was an excellent player and I needed little encouragement to join in. I played in several games with him and his Liverpool genius. Jackie Rankin lived for football, so he got on famously with Les. I had just started to go to school; the war was raging. Rationing of essential commodities created queues in most shops, but we all made do and mended anything that could have its useful life extended.

Our milk was delivered to the door by a pony and trap. It was contained within a large seventeen-gallon milk churn anchored inside the cart. Mother would allow me to visit the milkman, who would dip the ladle into the milk, filling the jug that I had carefully taken to him. Other general provisions were delivered by a large van, and I recall on one occasion we were desperately awaiting the delivery as we needed a clear glass shade for the oil lamp, without which we were struggling to see anything in the house once the curtains had to be drawn.

Damson Harvest

Our neighbours helped as far as they could. Our two neighbours and our family all pooled their efforts to harvest apples and damsons from the orchard in the early autumn. During the early forties we had a glut of damsons. We hadn't got sufficient boxes or tubs to put them in, so Mother cleaned out the water tub standing at the corner of the house, where it collected rain from the house roof, and it was filled with ripe damsons. My school lessons had included the techniques of winemaking in other countries, included the process whereby grapes were pressed by squashing them with your feet. I thought I would do the same. Mother caught me. No point in denying it – my legs up to my knees were purple. Mother wasn't pleased, but the neighbours saw the funny side of it and my only penalty was to have no socks for two days whilst Mother tried to remove the purple stain. Damson jam was hurriedly made by the bucketful.

Monday, Weekly Clothes-Wash Day

The NHS was still several years away – medical remedies were rooted in old-fashioned cures, and we were only too pleased to try some of them when we had the need to. Another practice was the complete disruption of the household on Mondays. This was the commonly accepted clothes-washing day. The coal fire worked overtime. We had to have hot water for the washing and the heat from the open fire to keep the solid-metal hand-operated irons red-hot to take out the creases from the wet clothes. All the wet clothes placed tremendous pressure on the lines, which as a result needed at least one large prop to prevent the washing from touching the ground. It was like a religion. Everyone washed clothes on a Monday. If it was wet the whole house had damp washing hanging everywhere. How did Mother ever survive? This is another memory to return to again much later and was the significant element I used to effect arrests in a late night / early morning case of the robbery of a taxi driver. Mother's daily fight for survival required Mother to drag her four children around to local farmhouses, where she would clean, scrub floors and do the weekly clothes washing. She would push the pram in all weathers, carrying my youngest brother with my two sisters and I scrambling along behind her.

House Brush and Gypsies

Mother's determination to keep her brood around her can be gleaned from her methods of instilling family discipline. The symbol of punishment was our house brush. It stood at the foot of the stairs in the living room, which, importantly, was the furthest point from the back door. I never realised the significance of this until much later in life. When we became too noisy she would suddenly make a hurried movement for the house brush. Usually my sisters would spot this and give the alarm by shouting instructions to get out of the house. We would all dash to the back door and disappear down the backyard into the orchard and scale the nearest apple tree. Mother never went beyond the back door, where she would brandish the house brush, waving it around over her head and shouting her displeasure at us all. A short time later we were allowed back into the house. It worked every time.

As I was the villain in the family she had a special way of dealing with me. During these war years the countryside was continually roamed by Gypsies. Some had ponies and carts; others walked with bulging bags of pegs and dolly stones – used for scrubbing the front and rear doorsteps and window sills of houses. Her ultimate weapon in maintaining discipline was to simply fill a pillowcase with old rags and make me stand outside the front door. I was to wait for the Gypsies to take me away with them. I screamed·continually. What I never realised was that she was stood in the front room, hiding behind the curtain, which was hanging behind the door as an insulator and draught excluder. I seemed to stand there for ages, straining every muscle in my body to catch the sound of approaching Gypsies and completely petrified just in case one came along. It worked. I only remember enduring this treatment a couple of times, but as I got to know Mother later in life I realised this example for me and the rest of her children was for her a most excruciating experience.

Grandparents

Sunday evening was a time when my grandmother (Dad's mother) would visit us. The back door would suddenly be flung open and in would walk the frightening image of an elderly woman. She would be wearing a black topcoat and hat and would sit in the fireside chair opposite Mother. She never spoke to my brother and me. When she did speak it was to Mother in a low whisper. After about an hour she would walk upstairs and visit each bedroom. We knew precisely where she was as her shoes clattered along the floorboards and her weight announced her progress on every stair. All four children sat in total silence side by side on the sofa until she suddenly rose from the chair and announced that she was leaving to catch the bus. I had to escort her to the bus stop, which was about a quarter of a mile from the house and along an unlit country lane. The bus would arrive about ten minutes later and we would stand together in complete silence. As the bus arrived she would suddenly turn to me and press a penny into my hand. Once she was on the bus I ran home, anxious to get rid of the penny as if it was a token of evil spirits, and waited for her next visit with continuing fear.

My other grandparents were equally abhorrent. Mother would take me on the bus and I would sit next to her crying my eyes out until we got to the front door of their house. I wasn't allowed to speak to them. Grandma would shout at me incessantly. Initially the only safe haven was to sit on her sofa, but I couldn't escape from her chastising about "Wipe that smirk off your face!" I hadn't a clue what a smirk was. I never dared to ask her. Granddad would announce his evening return from work with the echo and clatter of his hobnailed boots as he walked along the covered entrance to the back door. He would sit at the table and eat his evening meal – or tea, as we knew it. I vividly remembering watching him – or more precisely the bones of his lower jaw moving in a pronounced fashion as he devoured his meal.

But my salvation and my great delight was the sight of half a dozen hens in their backyard. This provided me with an escape plan. I would spend most of the day gathering grass and dandelion leaves to feed the hens. I was to later possess a dozen hens at my mother's house and spend ten years working with a dairy herd – perhaps Grandma's hens sparked the birth of this line of interest. Grandma would cook everything on the open fire as Mother did. But dinner (lunch) and tea were always accompanied by a dish of rice pudding. This was cooked on the open fire and she would somehow always have some remaining in the dish. Regularly throughout the day homeless people would knock on her door. She didn't have any money, but she provided food by way of the warmed-up rice pudding. It was eaten on the doorstep, where the empty dish was also left. It was an act of generosity that seemed to be prevalent during the 1940s, but it has been replaced in the twenty-first century by food banks, etc.

Much later in life she would visit my mother. This time I found her to be extremely pleasant and laughed at the least provocation. Maybe her sombre disposition was affected by the worry of her youngest child, Fred, who was always referred to by Mother as 'our Freddie'. He was serving in the Royal Navy, but would return home safely at the end of the war. My elder brother, after Dad's death, spent the remaining part of his early life with them.

Sirens and Blackouts

Mother was continually required to put the house into blackout mode. The town's siren could easily be heard inside the house, and it would trigger instant blackout action. During the night she would take us one by one out of our beds, carry us down the stairs and lie us, either totally asleep or half asleep, on the shelves in the pantry. The feeling of being woken from a deep sleep with only intimations of some impending disaster as she walked down the steep wooden stairs in total darkness with us tightly held in her arms was in itself terrifying. In the pitch-blackness the faint wail of the police-station siren could be heard outside and at any moment the feeling of being dropped and falling down the steep stairs was anticipated with dread. Mother would continually whisper to us to keep quiet and go back to sleep on the pantry shelf. Needless to say, we didn't have any food in the pantry which was a small room with solid walls on each side and was protected overhead by the wooden stairs. Once the all-clear was sounded she would repeat the process in reverse.

Thunderstorms presented other problems. We didn't have electricity in the house, but on hearing the first peal of thunder we would be catapulted into total panic. Every door in the house had to be opened wide as the expected thunderbolt would fall down the chimney and seek a way to the outside. If it got obstructed, the house would be burnt to the ground. Mother would often repeat tales of thunderbolts creating this panic and damage in houses in our home town. During these storms we lived in complete silence and terror, afraid that we could be struck and wiped out at any time.

Keeping the Home Fire Burning

Keeping the fire burning presented a constant challenge for Mother. It was simply no fire equals no heat, food or hot water; and whilst we didn't wash that frequently, doing so in cold water in the winter isn't recommended. Mother's self-reliance plan was twofold. We would be sent out on expeditions to collect sticks from nearby woods, and we would visit the cinder tip at the rear of Seddons salt factory as the workmen discharged the hot cinder waste after the coal had burnt to take the water element out of the brine, leaving pure white pans of salt.

During the winter of 1947 my sister Freda and I set out to cut wood in a nearby wood with what we were told was our father's axe. The large axe head was at the end of a yard-long handle. We only managed to collect sticks as all our efforts to chop up larger logs ended in failure. The snow was a couple of inches deep outside the wood, and the temperature was extremely cold. We were miserable and ultimately returned home with barely enough sticks to light the following day's fire. But if Mother was disappointed she never showed it.

Each time I went to pick the cinders there would be several

groups of women with children busy filling their sacks. They would tell us the best place to get the coke/coal. Sometimes one of the children would slip down the cinder heap as it was extremely steep and loose in parts. We would all stop picking and rush to help the stricken child. No one thought twice about their own safety. A warning was shouted across the cinder heap in unison by most of the pickers when the emptying process was about to begin. We would collect the cinders (coke) and carry home our gains in a sack. This was about a mile trek. Nevertheless this was more rewarding than trying to cut wood, so consequently we visited this cinder heap on many occasions.

Potato Picking

Potato-picking time was when many families would come together, visit local farms and get the potatoes gathered. A shire horse was used to draw the potato digger, and we would take up our positions along the potato row. Once the digger had passed, we moved forward and feverishly pitched the potatoes into baskets or hampers. It was back-breaking work. Time went quickly – conversations amongst neighbours never seemed to wane, and the wonderment of the huge horse puffing and blowing, with a rolling gait, swinging from side to side as he dragged the digger behind him, left many of us wide-eyed.

Our big treats were at the end of the day. We would be lifted on to the back of this huge animal. We clung on to him as he slowly made his way to the farmyard. As his harness chains jangled, his huge feet paced slowly and purposefully in a measured way, steadily enough for us, his young charges, to confidently chatter on the horse's back until we arrived in the farmyard. We were allowed to take potatoes home and the children were given sixpence each for the day by the farmer. Farm labour was in short supply. Men were still doing war duties and most people had no appetite for it as they could find easier jobs that were less exposed to the vagaries of bad weather. Their daily pay was derisory, but beggars couldn't be choosers. Some benefits for us children were that we were given a conducted tour of the farm buildings, and the variety of farm animals was always of great interest to us.

At eleven years of age I was allowed ten days away from school (two weeks) to help farmers with their potato harvest. To control and monitor this, my teacher gave me a green card with twenty divisions printed on it each representing half a day. The farmer would sign each half-day section as confirmation of my attendance. This work cemented my relations with many of our neighbouring farmers, but once the war had ended the scheme ceased. I was the last recipient of this two-week potato-picking holiday in my home town. Similar to cinder picking, many neighbours gathered to assist in the harvest. This collective process enhanced and strengthened the neighbourly fibre in their bodies. Crime appeared non-existent – the back doors to our houses were never locked. All this would disappear, but those involved would never forget.

An Enemy Agent

American troops occupied an airbase near to our village and it became obvious that they were a target for enemy planes. The route of the lorry convoys passed close by our house, but they were required to stop at the crossroads. Their approach could easily be heard inside our house. I would sit on the black-and-white painted railings, and shout and wave to the American troops. Initially they would throw packets of chewing gum out to me. I tried one packet, but never repeated the practice. My brothers and sisters, however, chewed it with relish. To get an opportunity to get more gum I repositioned the fingerpost road sign so that it would be another mile before the driver realised he had taken the wrong turn. The troops quickly realised who the villain was. They shouted in good humour at me, and on approaching the crossroads again they threw out more packets of gum. The local cycle stockist (Ken Foster) was kept busy supplying bikes to the troops and their support staff, which gave them an opportunity to invade our small town and perhaps some relief from fighting the war.

Knitting, Carol-Singing, the Wireless and the Granddaughter Clock

Birthdays, Christmas and New Year were always celebrated with home cooking, toys and more practical items, such as clothing – and in my case I knitted a scarf. It finished three times wider that it started. It wasn't my best work, but I had to wear it. My brother and sisters knitted gloves and together we would sew pieces of rag on to a hessian backing to make rugs. We would all visit our neighbours and sing our versions of Christmas carols. All of them would stand at the door whilst we sang and gave us money and apples harvested earlier in the year from their orchards. A poignant memory that floods into my mind is of the smell that enveloped us as we stood at the front door being greeted by all the occupants. Apples harvested the previous autumn were being stored inside these houses. As each door opened, the rich mellowness of the ripening fruit grabbed our noses even in the coldest of weathers. We were never allowed to leave without accepting a paper bag bulging with their toils, which as if by magic would somehow find a way into our Christmas-morning stockings. This ritual was as important to our neighbours as Christmas was to us. These half a dozen bedraggled children must have been a heart-rending sight. In my case holes in the darned elbows of my jacket were accompanied by holes in the darned heels of my socks, portraying the daily battle Mother had keeping us all in one piece. After the carol-singing each one would be questioned, without realising it, so that each neighbour could monitor our growing lives and get an appreciation of how we were managing to exist in these difficult times.

One of our neighbours had a crab-apple tree that had ripe fruit before any other fruit trees. I would climb through the hedge, through an established hole, and fill my pockets. On reflection I believe these neighbours were well aware of my exploits, but never mentioned it when they met me at other times.

Our accumulator battery-powered wireless was our only contact with the outside world. We used it most sparingly and once it began to run flat I had to leave it at the electric shop on my way to school and collect it on the way home fully charged – charge, one penny. Our only clock was positioned on the living-room wall. The noise of the swinging pendulum rarely penetrated the noise we made, but if it stopped Mother would swoop on it to either rebalance or rewind it. The rebalancing of it as it hung on the wall was always a most delicate process. Sometimes it would take her ages to restore the balance, and during the time when we didn't know the correct time we relied on the wireless.

Electricity came to our cottage in the late forties, and whilst we only had a light fitted to the living room and Mother's bedroom it was to herald a brighter existence for us all, quickly evidenced when Mother was granted the keys to a new council house in the town.

CHAPTER 2

SCHOOL

My first warning of attending school was announced by my eldest sister, Gwen. Unless I could spell and write my own name and address I would be sent home. She continually ensured that I mastered this particular task. The kitchen table was put to full use and both sisters, Gwen and Freda, piled on the pressure until they were sure that I could virtually write my name and address blindfold.

On my first day at school we all stood in the living room with the back door open so that we could hear the approaching bus some two miles away. We all had two pennies: one penny fare each way. It was a time of great excitement. We always sat on the lower deck and the conductor helped us to jump from the bus at the Bull Ring in the town centre. School dinners were devoured as if we had never eaten food. In the afternoons we all had to sleep on fold-up beds. Curtains at the windows in the assembly hall were drawn closed, firstly to make sure we slept and secondly because air raids were becoming commonplace and the curtains would give us some protection against flying glass. All our teachers were females. They were strict, but also kind to everyone.

When school time finished I would meet up with my elder sister Freda and we would catch the bus back home. We waited in the Bull Ring for the bus and stood outside the front display window of Fittons, the butchers. There was never much meat hanging on the hooks, but they made a great display of their home-baked pies. There was a choice of two: meat and potato or meat. I stood under the shop's awning, my nose pressed against the window, and wondered what they would taste like. We never got to try one because we didn't have any money. Some days the bus was late, but what did it matter? I continued to stand motionless, watching customers enter and select their pies. Throughout our early life our neighbours – the Bostocks – tolerated a great deal of noise from our family. They never complained. Furthermore, they were always there to swop any items of food rations to stave off hunger as we all tried to get through each week.

Moving to junior school in the middle forties was a wake-up call. Playtime was over. I struggled with all my lessons, but I had two excellent teachers: Miss Haynes and Miss Gee. There were three classes, each with at least thirty children, in each year. For some unknown reason they succeeded in keeping me in their A stream.

If we had heavy snowfall our bus would be taken out of service and we had to walk home. Several times we trudged in three-foot snowdrifts, but we never missed a day at school. Mother was working at the ICI factory in Middlewich, which meant that my younger brother and I would be the first of the family to be returning home at the end of the day. We didn't have a key to the back door – it wasn't locked – and we quickly became experts at starting the coal fire, often watching it until others returned home. Harsh winters made it difficult for Mother to keep our fire going, and 1947 was a particularly severe winter. Leaving school at the end of the day, I was forced to walk home as the buses had been taken off the road. As I got near to our house I had to walk up Spittle Hill. Someone had cleared a path through the snow which was just wide enough to allow a person to walk through. With snow piled high on each side and unable to see over the top, my younger brother and I slowly made our way through until we got to the top of the hill. At times the wind would swirl any loose snow and create a mini snowstorm. This made visibility poor. It was too icy to run and on those occasions we were always glad to get home.

Living in this rural community may have had its drawbacks, but we all clung together in the warmth of that fire glowing in the hearth, and four noisy children were quickly satisfied with a slice of toast laced with hot butter/dripping fat. We didn't care as we were home and warm again.

Coke Run

Mother's plan was to dispatch me with the old pram to the gasworks at our neighbouring town, about four miles away. This pram would have been used by all of the children and was now to be put to another use. Early on a Saturday morning I would set off on this expedition. I was to queue at the gasworks in Winsford and wait for the coke to be shovelled into the bag Mother had made certain was in the pram. There were always other adults in the queue. Everyone was dressed in dark clothing – usually heavy overcoats, gloves, hats and clogs. The air was thick with smoke and fumes from a variety of small industries which over the years had blackened the appearance of many buildings. This was an awful town, but the sombre scene was further complicated by the terrain as the gasworks was in the centre of the town and near to the River Weaver. Therefore to succeed on their journey home with their heavy bags of coke everyone was required to overcome a steep hill.

There were five steep hills, all describing a similar incline out of the town centre. If this assembled queue had been anxious about their return journeys they didn't show it. This bunch of resilient souls, irrespective of the weather, were continually laughing and talking to each other, catching up on local gossip, and before very long it seemed the man in charge was beckoning to me to move forward. Whilst I wasn't part of the continuous chat and banter, the person immediately behind me had made sure I knew they would help me get loaded and safely on my return journey. The tricky part was to ensure the large bag of coke was balanced inside the pram in such a way that it didn't tip forward or backwards, which would allow the bag to slide off the pram. The first ten yards or so I was escorted by a person from the queue, and when they were satisfied that I could manage the load they returned to their place in the queue. This was the community cohesiveness shared by many during these war years and immediately afterwards. Once I had the forward momentum I didn't look back. I knew my return journey would challenge every muscle in my body, but the sooner I got started the quicker I would get home. The hill climbing out of Winsford and towards Middlewich was extremely steep to an eleven-or-twelve-year-old boy and it often forced me to take half a step at a time until I made it to the top. As it was early on a Saturday morning it was a task I always seemed to carry out without any other people being about. If the bag of coke slipped or I in some way or other lost control of the pram I would be on my own. I knew I wouldn't be able to lift the bag back into the pram, so the struggle was entirely mine. There was no alternative. I had to get the coke home.

Halfway home was a sweet shop. Armed with four two-ounce coupons, I bought sweets for Gwen, Freda and Allan. My boiled sweets (pear drops) were mostly eaten before I got home, but on arriving home my brother and sisters would cheer loudly. We all celebrated as we knew the importance of this fuel to our existence. This wasn't a weekly task as the next journey would be determined by the reliability of coal deliveries, usually disrupted by extremely cold and snowy conditions. Maintaining that fire in the grate in our household was essential to sustain our well-being.

My Dog, Toby

When we arrived home from school one day, Mother announced that she had got a dog for us. We named him Toby, and he must have only been about three months old. We gave him a wooden box as his bed in the shed next to the house and we took him around to all the neighbours. They loved him. Training him to do anything was difficult, but traffic on the road outside our cottage was extremely light, which gave us plenty of warning when to get this uncontrollable bundle of energy back to the lead.

After about three months he became ill and wouldn't eat his food. Many neighbours visited and brought with them their herbal remedies. None worked. It may be prudent to dwell on the word 'neighbours', because they were also friends and their friendship cut across any divide created by social class. This gave me a greater understanding of human relations, which became a central theme later in my story. About a week later Toby died. I had to dig the grave in our back garden, carry him to it and bury him. Mother supervised, but it was a very sad time. I didn't realise or appreciate it at the time, but it seemed that all our neighbours were in mourning, and for several months afterwards they would interrupt their journey to visit our house or stop and talk to me about Toby.

Family Illness (Allan Is Paralysed, Freda Goes to Hospital and Gwen Faints in School Assembly)

Without warning of what was to come we all started to get out of bed one morning when my younger brother, Allan, started screaming at the top of his voice. Mother appeared instantly and was probably expecting to shout at me as most of the trouble in the house usually rested with me. She was surprised that Allan was in such great pain. He was paralysed. To touch him caused great pain. Mother applied her usual herbal lotion and carried him to the sofa in the living room. She persisted with this move although he carried on screaming. She wasn't going to leave him in bed on his own. Once settled, he ate breakfast and stayed on the sofa all day. When we went to bed I was given strict instructions not to touch him.

The following day Mother placed the wireless on a chair in the backyard. Allan and I listened to the 1947 FA Cup Final between Burnley and Charlton. Both Allan and I were staunch supporters of Burnley. They lost 1–0. It was a sunny and warm afternoon and Allan's pain seemed to be receding.

The following day he had recovered, but for several days he was made to sit on a chair in the backyard. No one ever explained what the cause of this sudden illness was. It came and went quickly and never returned. As it was pre-NHS, calling on the services of the Doctor wasn't an option as we didn't have any money to pay him.

Poor living and sanitary conditions seemed to be affecting us all. My elder sister Freda suddenly disappeared as Mother had her whisked off into a hospital suffering from scarlet fever. The house went into mourning again. Conversations were subdued, but we did at least keep the curtains drawn back and off the windows.

When I arrived home from school one day, Mother announced to us that she had a surprise. She opened the door leading to the parlour and Freda appeared. Everyone cheered and shouted with relief and joy.

One morning at assembly the usual noise of 300 pupils suddenly hushed. The whispering between the other pupils was that someone had fainted. It was Gwen, my eldest sister. She was taken to the staffroom, so I left the assembly to visit her. The Doctor prescribed a small white pill that she had to take every day. It must have been a most harrowing experience for Gwen, but she seemed to take it in her stride. The next day she was back at school as though nothing had happened.

The war was becoming a memory, but our family illnesses reminded us of our own vulnerabilities.

John Charles Simmonds (JC)

Before this incident in 1946 Mother got married again, to John Charles Simmonds, a native of South Wales who at the time was a serving officer in the RAF stationed at Byley. JC was the first father I had known. He was at work most of the time, but he found the time to present our case to the council for one of their new houses in the town. Our sister Ellen Anne was born in 1947.

We moved to our new house sometime later. What a difference! Hot and cold water upstairs and downstairs, three bedrooms, a bathroom, two toilets and an electric supply in every room. Joy was unbounded. It was like moving into a palace. The old pram was to be used once more. Mother filled it with pots and pans and other fragile items, such as the wall clock and the paraffin lamp. We were all sad to leave the old place, but we had outgrown it and the reality was that to us the new council house was sheer luxury. The living conditions in the old cottage were a health hazard and needed an upgrade to bring them into the twentieth century.

After three or four trips with the pram, Mother and I set about cleaning the new house. After sweeping away builders' dust and mopping the floors we searched for any food or brewing materials that we had previously packed in the pram. In amongst the dust and debris on the floor I found a half-crown. Mother decided that fish and chips from the town's chip shop were called for. During our makeshift meal, eaten from newspaper wrappings, Mother recalled some of her memories about her time at Stanthorne. She was keen to impress on me that before she had left on that last morning she had visited our neighbours the Bostocks. It was the first time she had visited these neighbours, although throughout the war years we had exchanged tea, sugar, butter, cheese, etc. (usually carried out by her children). She took great pride in telling me as we sat on the window sill of our new council house that she had never had a wrong word with them and for that reason she was sad to be leaving. JC's addition to the family had had a positive effect. We gained a sister and his efforts raised all of our living and health standards. Sadly he was struck down with TB and spent a great deal of time in hospital. He died in March 1958.

Arthur Mort, Milkman

In 1949 I was to meet the first of many inspirational people that influenced my life; and like the others, he became so without it initially registering. One Saturday morning I was playing football outside our new house when an old milk van stopped. The driver, Arthur Mort, walked across the road to me and asked if I would like to help him deliver milk to our neighbours. I agreed, but he insisted that he got permission from Mother. I carried on until dinner time, then returned early the following morning to help with deliveries throughout the town. It was a great job. I quickly got familiar with the geography of the town, the names of his customers and their requirements. It would take us about two hours to complete the daily milk round – longer on Saturdays and Sundays because we collected money from the customers – then we would bottle the fresh milk ready for the next day's deliveries.

Milk bottles were still made of glass. In the winter months this made handling them a very cold job, but running from door to door quickly generated body heat which slowly percolated down to the fingers. Another effect of delivering glass milk bottles to houses along these quiet village streets was that my presence was clearly heralded by the chinking full bottles as I set them down and as I chinked the empty ones to return them to the van for recharging with milk back at the dairy. Arthur would insist on a chat and visiting a café in the town so that we could have a cup of tea and eat the half-coated chocolate shortbread biscuit he always bought. He became interested in my school lessons and quickly realised that I had failed my eleven-plus exam. He also became aware that my inability to communicate with my teachers was highlighting other problems. I was a complete failure at maths, and my exam results reflected this. In one of our conversations he revealed that he and his wife had recently retired. Both had been school teachers. From that moment on the price of a bottle of milk, times the number of bottles, times the number of days the customer had received them was a total I had to work out in my head, then obtain the correct payment from the customer. There were numerous times when I would stand on a customer's doorstep still trying to work out the correct money that I should receive. Some of them helped me out at first, but Arthur's methods were working. He had made the whole learning process enjoyable by making sure we laughed at my mistakes. On a daily basis, once we got into the morning milk round I would get interrogated as he needed to determine which problems we were discussing in class. He was concerned that I wasn't confident enough to challenge the teacher over any area of a current problem I found difficultly with. His strategy was to encourage me to be more involved. I never realised it, but he was trying to develop my social skills. Delivering milk to numerous customers and complying with their wishes, usually by having a short conversation on the doorstep was the first step in building confidence.

He insisted that I engaged in conversations with my teachers and made the observation that teachers were unlikely to dwell over what I regarded as stumbling blocks to solving a problem unless I went out of my way to challenge existing unfathomable problems. He encouraged me to understand the basic requirements of communication. His message was simple: unless I asked I would always remain in the dark. Although it was simple advice I didn't find it easy. He was aware of my shortcomings and continued to question my progress and any conversations I had in my maths class. He was ruthless in pursuing his rationale, simply repeating, "If you don't ask you will never know."

The next class exam proved to be an eye-opener. Usually I

occupied one of the last couple of places in my class of thirty plus, but that was to come to an abrupt end. Our maths teacher always read out the results, with pupils who had the best results being mentioned first. Everyone dreaded this part of the lesson, but I wasn't prepared for what was to follow. In his usual commanding voice our maths teacher started to read the results.

"The third highest mark was achieved by . . ."

Pencils remained poised over exercise books. No one moved. We were all staring at the teacher; he was deliberately looking around the class and not at any particular pupil. Why was he hesitating? Had he made a mistake in compiling his list? I dreaded this theatre, even though I wasn't really interested as my goal was to try to keep out of the last three. My mind drifted to the feeling of dread when he got to his concluding remarks, which would be about the right time for my name to be read out amongst my classmates who regularly occupied the lowest positions.

After what seemed to be a very long pause he continued. He called out my name. The whole class looked at me. 'It must be a mistake,' I thought, but to make matters worse our teacher stood for several seconds and repeated the result, mentioning my name again. Maybe he couldn't believe it – I certainly didn't and neither did any of my classmates. The teacher was clearly delighted and proud of his efforts to be part of my conversion. In fact he was more excited than I was.

The following day I ran all the way to the dairy to start my milk round. Arthur stood by the van, which was loaded and ready for the start of the morning deliveries. I spluttered my jumbled and probably incoherent message, which he seemed to understand. He was also clearly delighted. He maintained his insistence that every problem could be solved by approaching it systematically and by using the formulae he had drilled into me. His first step was to get my opinion about what I thought the answer would be, then patiently work through the details. He was really keen on my relationships with all the teachers and that I had the mental ability to formulate a close approximation of the right answer. He had made the all-important breakthrough.

It had been my lucky day when Arthur asked for my help to deliver his milk. My school career improved dramatically, not just because in the learning process I had lost the fear about maths problems, which knocked on and equated to an improved ability and confidence to converse with the teachers. Later I would be tested again and, clearly not having lost this new-found ability, excelled again in the police entrance and educational exams.

Still at school, my interest in gardening seemed to give me the edge over my other classmates and I managed to win the gardening prize for at least three years. Mr Mathias was responsible for this. I found him extremely interesting and easy to get on with, replicating the same personal interest demonstrated by Arthur Mort. We organised the school garden and cropping programme together. He later became the school's head teacher. He wasn't a good teacher – he was a *great* teacher.

For my final eighteen months I was the head boy at my school. This progress stemmed from the initial efforts of Arthur Mort. His patience and belief in me had transformed my outlook on life. My confidence had grown dramatically. I stopped walking the other way when approached by teachers, and even entered into conversations with them. The final two or three years at school had been most enjoyable and turned on the chance meeting one Saturday morning with our milkman. It was his and Mother's belief that I should get involved, and it was Arthur's way of repaying my mother for having a belief in him as the stranger in town by allowing me to help him out in his hour of need. That fateful meeting as I crashed the football into the side of his milk van was all that it took to make changes in my life. That moment came unexpectedly, without warning, and could so easily have been lost, and like most young lads I paid very little heed to it at the time.

CHAPTER 3

FARM LABOURER AT BROOK HOUSE AND KINDERTON HALL FARMS

There was nothing unusual about returning home after school. Mother was preparing a meal for us all and at this period of time because my two older sisters were working we had our meals separately. As she was busy in the kitchen she mentioned that a local dairy farmer was advertising for a farm labourer. It was almost Christmas and in a couple of weeks, at the end of 1951, I was leaving school. Sister Gwen had left school at fourteen years of age, but changes within the educational system meant I was to finish my schooldays on attaining fifteen years. Within ten minutes I was stood knocking on the back door of Brook House Farm.

Lassie

As I approached I was ambushed by a black-and-white collie dog. She didn't bark. She cautiously got nearer with her tail wagging furiously. I stroked her head and she remained with me until the maid answered and ushered me into the living room. An hour later after meeting with my future employer she was sat waiting for me at the back door. I wasn't to realise it, but I had just had two of the most important encounters of my life.

John Edward Lea, Farmer

John Lea and his wife, Alice, were sat in front of a large open fire and between them was the baby bath and a young baby who was obviously intent on removing all the bathwater on to the tiled floor. John had a generous physique, fair hair, a soft voice with a distinctive high pitch and a firm handshake. For fifteen minutes he determined where I was living, the number of brothers and sisters I had and my school record. I was to start as soon as possible, which was delayed a week because of Christmas, but he made me aware that on my first morning he would be waiting to introduce me to his other staff.

I had just met a very inspirational, courageous family man. His farm dog was to become my shadow and play a pivotal role in my future existence. John and his family would later move from Brook House Farm to Kinderton Hall Farm after the death of his parents, and I was to remain with him until 1959.

There were three other workers at Brook House Farm. One had been with John for forty years, lived in one of his tied cottages and would retire about three years later. He typified the old farmworker of the day. Together with his wife they would walk to the town once a week and spend a week in Blackpool as their annual holiday. He didn't drive a car or ride a bike. As far as they were concerned nothing existed beyond this world. He wore traditional country clothes, which comprised hobnailed boots and corduroy breeches with ankle-to-knee leather gaiters. His lifetime working in the country had left him with a weather-beaten face with bright eyes that peered out from under the flat cap and through his bushy eyebrows. His cap appeared glued to his head.

My main role was to assist with the dairy herd. I found working with animals absorbing and John's light-touch management style allowed everyone to develop, help each other and in doing so gain tremendous experience as the other farmworkers gladly shared their skills and experiences.

Close to Nature

I started my job in January 1952 and quickly realised that working with animals and close to nature was tremendously rewarding. Maybe not all the time, as I discovered when I was tasked with harvesting several acres of turnips in January which still clung on to the previous night's frost! For several weeks during the afternoon I set about harvesting this root crop so that I could put them through the mincing machine for our dairy cows. As light faded each day, different flocks of birds would fly overhead as they made their way to their night roosts. In the early fifties these would include swirling flocks of noisy starlings regularly heading for night-time roosts, in their favourite trees. Lapwings (peewits) would cartwheel overhead and skim the ground, but the robin was the most vociferous in totally bare hedgerows whilst an occasional hare would lope over the rows of turnips, only casting a fleeting look towards me without altering his stride. As dusk and fading light began to reign supreme in this rural scene the intense cold constantly reminded me that my hardest lesson was trying to endure the intense cold.

My final journey at the end of the day was to walk back to the milking sheds to rejoin my other colleagues. I was greeted on this short walk by the silent flying brigade – namely, our barn inhabitants who were going out on their nightly patrols to mop up any errant mice and any airborne moths. I think the owls and bats took it in turns to skim as close as they could to my head as if they were playing games.

I usually met John on a Friday evening, when he would make it his job to see all the men from both farms (a total of nine), deliver individual wages and discuss all our farming issues. There were other times when we would be working together, when he confirmed my initial view that he wasn't your everyday farmer as he developed a unique interest in his staff, their families and their well-being. Our weekly meetings and discussions wouldn't be drawn out as everyone looked forward to the weekend and wanted to go home. John would use the opportunity to plan the following week, and on one occasion he asked me to visit Kinderton Hall Farm and work on a particular job with his horse manager.

Jim 'Tiger' Smith, Horse Manager and Countryman

I was to work with Jim 'Tiger' Smith, who was specifically in charge of the three shire horses. Tiger was in his mid thirties, married with three children, living in another one of John's tied cottages, and had been in his present position for many years. He was heavily built with black hair receding from his forehead. His huge sideburns seemed to meet under his chin. He always wore a red-with-white-spots neck scarf and his red checks gave him the appearance of a Gypsy. He was exceptionally talented in country and animal matters, always accompanied by two Irish wolfhounds, which would obediently sit for hours outside any building that he was in and would walk about five yards behind him as he walked around the farm. I soon learnt that he had a singing voice that Mario Lanza would have yearned for. On occasions he instructed me to bring the shire horses from their pasture to the stables. He handed a bucket of bran to me to help me place the bridle on to one of them as he said the others would then follow.

Humiliated by Three Shire Horses

My first experience with horses was one to forget: I was attacked by three huge horses. They came towards me, then at the last moment, before they collided with me, they spun around and kicked their back legs into the air. The bran in the bucket had been devoured and they were intent on staying in their pasture and frightening the living daylights out of me. After about fifteen minutes of my miserable efforts, which ended in complete failure, I walked back to see Tiger. He was not a happy man and in no uncertain terms told me to follow him. As he approached the horses he called out to them. They lifted their heads and, as if marching in time, they walked slowly to the entrance gate. Once the gate was opened they followed Tiger in single file and ended their journey by standing in their own stalls. I was witnessing a master at work.

I was then given a lesson in horse management. My ability to communicate with the horses was woeful. I was made to release the horses, return them to their stables and move them from one side of their stalls to the other. It was a great levelling experience as they persisted in doing their own thing, with Tiger sat on a bale of straw watching and listening to my every command and move. Here was a man who had received a limited education, but his knowledge of the countryside, animals and particularly his dogs was exceptional. With animals he was gentle but firm. His relationship with the shire horses was awe-inspiring. He generously gave his time to demonstrate his easy knack of moving huge animals, regardless of their own individual characters and independent minds, and made it look as if by some miracle they completely understood and obeyed his every verbal command and physical gesture. He was also testing my temperament, patience and suitability to handle his horses. We engaged in arable work with the horses, which was physically taxing, but he was scrutinising my management and handling of his horses. He also taught me the art of ploughing with a single-furrow horse-drawn plough. He demanded throughout that I spoke to the horse continually, asking if I could see the horse's ears and were they turned towards me as I struggled with the plough? At a later date this was an experience I would rely on to prevent schoolchildren from receiving serious injuries as they crossed a main road at the end of their school day.

Taking an Early Bath

John decided that he would drain the pool at the front of the hall to remove all the overgrown reeds. Several of us attended, placed scaffolding-type planks of wood on top of the reeds and began the process of digging the reeds out of the pond. None of the staff had ever done this job previously, so there was a certain amount of excitement in the air as we gathered to make inroads into this job.

The planks quickly became wet and slippery, and the inevitable happened: it was Tiger who slipped into the reeds, immediately disappearing up to his waist. Initially we were alarmed for his safety, but our mood quickly turned to one of ridicule and humour when we had safely got him secured to the metal drag forks that we had decided to use. To drain the pond a sluice gate was opened so that the level of water reduced to a stream running through the middle.

We didn't find many fish in the pond except for about four of five large pike. They were about three foot long with huge jaws and inward-slanting teeth – not fish to mess with! Pike are extremely proficient predators, taking other fish and young waterfowl. They looked so frightening that getting a yard away from a dead one was for me close enough.

There are two other practices that we engaged in that seem to belong to a long-gone era. (1) The advent of spring was always announced by the arrival of our mole catcher. He would set his traps across wide areas of the two farms, returning later to see what success he had had. He was paid on the number of moles he had caught, so on retrieving the traps that had snared the unfortunate ones their dead carcases were hooked on to the barbed-wire boundary fences. (2) Each year a proportion of our arable acres were sown with cereal crops. A portion of these cereal crops were undersown with clover and grass seed. Once these crops had been drilled into the soil, the fiddle would be used. This was basically a canvas bag holding the seeds mounted on to a board with a slot in the base to allow the seeds to drop. A wheel at the base of the bag was connected by small cogs which when turned, pulled the seeds to the spinning cog and cascaded them on to the soil. The actual amount of seed being sown was determined by the person moving the distribution cog in a movement resembling a musician playing the fiddle. The 'fiddler' would walk at an even pace, but in tune with his arm movement so as to deliver an even amount of the required seed on to the ground. In our case once the binder had cut the corn and bundled it into sheaves, next year's crop for our hay harvest could be seen.

Derek Evans, Ballroom Dancing

Derek was a member of the team at the hall. We were the same age and had much in common. One of Derek's ideas was to go ballroom dancing. Two more unlikely lads you could never have imagined. I instantly gave him the thumbs down. I was a farm worker wearing clogs and ankle spats. They were not likely to fit naturally with any activities on a dance floor. I couldn't see how I could make the conversion, but he was not to be dissuaded.

One Monday evening Derek and another friend visited our

house. Mother gave me fifteen minutes to be on my bike and ready to cycle with the others. Disobeying her was not an option. My introduction to ballroom dancing was about to begin. Al Martino, Alma Cogan and Frankie Vaughan (whom I was to meet later at Buckingham Palace) were popular singers in the charts at that time. Derek would lead the gang in singing continuously as we cycled to the dancing school and on the return journey.

The manageress/proprietress of this dancing school was a forceful lady and her options to get out of the lessons were non-existent. This was a twelve-month experience, during which I mastered several dances, totally mystifying my brothers and sisters and during which I gained a dancing partner. She was selected for me by the dancing-school instructor. She was an extremely good dancer, but I had to practice dancing steps at every opportunity; otherwise I would be letting the group down. The doubled-sided cowshed for sixty cows had a four-foot-wide central pathway. This was an ideal space which I am sure entertained the girls (cows) as their big eyes followed my every move as I twirled and clattered my steel-tipped clogs over the concrete surface. My dancing partner was younger than me and we didn't engage in much conversation so I got to know extremely little about her. I did, however, know that her name was Elizabeth Davies and her older sister always accompanied her. Derek and other gang members drifted away from the dancing school as they started courting, and this seemed to be the right time for me to seek different horizons. Many years later I was to fleetingly meet Elizabeth again (see Chapter 6) when I was in the company of the manager of a tennis tournament. Much to my shame and embarrassment, I didn't recognise her.

Philosophy in the Hay Harvest

Back on the farm, in the fifties the mechanisation revolution, interrupted by the war, was becoming evident once more in the countryside. Shire horses were less popular as tractors and a myriad of implements were demonstrating that they were less labour-intensive and able to deliver a much greater output. We were on the cusp of the agricultural revolution. The Massey Ferguson tractor was replacing many of the old wartime metal-rim-wheeled tractors, but there were to be casualties. Later a former Wythenshawe Hospital chairman organised a competition amongst his 5,000 staff, inviting entries of poems on any subject. My entry with an agricultural flavour was selected as the winner, with the winning entry to be displayed for twelve months on the hospital noticeboard.

John had purchased a hay baler. We said goodbye to the huge haystacks, and the combine harvester finally gave the death knell to the threshing machine. I always dreaded the arrival of the threshing machine. Usually it was a wintertime task as the machine would be drawn alongside the giant corn stacks stored in the farmyard barns. The corn sheaves were passed to a person on top of the machine to begin the process of separating the sheaves so that they could be fed into the drum. A total of six men would be needed to complete the operation. It was work often done in blinding dust, with a great deal of noise, with some roles open to the extremes of the weather. The haymaking harvest also changed dramatically. John had nominated me to assist him. He would arrive in the hayfield around mid morning and we would discuss the state of readiness of hay baling for that day.

On one occasion he had brought a can of tea. We drank it as we sat on a bale of hay. During the conversation we discussed my future plans. I had that sinking feeling that he wanted to get rid of me. In fact the opposite was the case, but he wanted me to seriously consider joining the police service. He was set in his opinion and wanted me to visit the police station that evening. I didn't, but he was to raise the subject several times. His belief that I had a different role in life was the trademark of this remarkable man.

The Tolpuddle Spirit

About this time I had been approached to be the union representative for the National Union of Agricultural Workers. Taking a break during haymaking, John and I sat on a hay bale in the middle of the field. We discussed the issue of the farm workers' union. I expected him to be unimpressed, but his response was most surprising. He urged me to do anything I could to help my fellow workers, and wanted me to discuss with him any problems that I thought he could help to resolve. He clearly didn't have a very high opinion of some of his fellow farmers. It was a subject we returned to several times over the next two years, and it gave me a greater insight into the reasons why his older staff were a contented team and had worked for him over many years. Resonating throughout our conversations was John's opinion about interactions with other people. My initial reactions were one of disbelief – I didn't believe him – but this slowly changed as I realised the immaturity of my views and that he earnestly believed in his. His basic philosophy was that he always treated other people as he hoped they would treat him if roles were reversed. He would often repeat that in our conversations, and he was never too busy to stop and chat over any farming or family-related issues. That advice has never left me.

CHAPTER 4

CRAZED BULL AT BROOK HOUSE FARM

Deadly Combat

What was to unfold was a life or death incident, but it didn't resemble the Battle of Middlewich, where in March 1643 Sir Thomas Aston's forces were decisively beaten by the Parliamentarians under Sir William Brereton. Kinderton Hall was used as Aston's headquarters and was largely undamaged. Unfortunately St Michael's Church, the imposing landmark in the heart of Middlewich, sustained structural damage where it is believed lives were lost. An epitaph, however, near to the priest's door reads, 'Here lies Anne wife of Daniel Barker who died July 3rd 1778 age 77. Some have children some have none But here lies the mother of twenty one.'

The last Monday in November 1957 had a chill in the air. Mist lingered in the hollows of our undulating fields. Leafless hawthorn hedges were dripping with excessive dew and the countryside seemed to sense early signs of winter yet to come. But that was to be expected so late in the year. Earlier that morning I had let the dozen or so ducks out of their night shed and I watched them as they trooped off to the brook in their usual style, waddling in single file and telling everyone of their delight to have been released for a day foraging amongst the weeds and depths of the water in the brook. There were no clues about what was to unfold that day. Nothing could have prepared us for what was shortly to happen. Our dairy herd were spending a limited time in the pastures and were being fed with winter fodder – kale that I had cut the previous day. The kale would be devoured gleefully and quickly by our cows, which had earlier been confined to their sheds overnight. I was in the orchard cleaning the farm's large hen cabin. Lassie would have been in her usual place, sitting outside the cabin.

It would have been around 10 a.m. when suddenly there was a loud crashing sound coming from the direction of the main road (A54). The hen cabin was about sixty yards away from it, and initially I thought vehicles had collided. Running into the adjacent field I was amazed to find one of our bulls had broken out of his meadow. He stood looking at me with steam billowing skywards from all over his body. The lack of wind and the chill in the air gave the scene an unreal feeling. The still morning air had been shattered by him destroying the five-barred gate that controlled access to the field, reducing it to firewood. To get to the farm from his meadow he would have demolished several other field gates, but the question I was asking myself was why? I realised that this was the same bull I had walked to a meadow about a mile away from the farm. John had convinced me that a leading pole with the hook through his nose was sufficient to control him and that I was completely safe as he said the bull was as 'soft as putty'. I had been relieved to get him to the meadow and release him to join about thirty young cows on that warm spring morning, jostling with his new friends. The change in him now was difficult to comprehend. He was much more mature and with a bigger body. His two horns, each at least a foot long, in any other setting would make him look a majestic animal, but as he faced me he looked terrifying. There was a moment when we just stood and stared at each other. I reminded myself that this was the gentle animal who just over six months earlier had allowed me to lead him along a main road, but he was now standing defiantly in the field, refusing to move in any direction. His defiance was exaggerated as he reared on to his back legs and crashed his two front legs into the ground accompanied by a deep and low growling noise. If there was a chill on the air that morning it hadn't registered with me.

I tried to usher him to a gate giving access to the farm buildings, but he didn't move one step. Instead he dipped his head, continued to growl and threatened to charge. Several times I questioned myself about his identity, but there was no mistake. It was the same animal, but I had never heard him growl with this low continuous noise similar to what I would have expected from a lion. What had changed him? But probably more to the point, what had caused this change? Why had he become so violent, destructive and threatening? He refused all my attempts to coax him to the gate, and because of his obvious hostility towards me I stayed about twenty yards away from him. We were at stalemate. I was unsure about getting any closer to him – he was obviously warning me off. How was I going to break this impasse?

Suddenly I heard John's voice. He was shouting at me from the shattered gate. He had got out of his car and asked me to get a couple of pitchforks. I returned from the farm buildings and gave him a pitchfork; I had a leading pole with a hook on one end to clip through the ring in the nose of the bull. This was the pole I had used six months or so earlier. I wedged open the farm gate as I re-entered the field as the plan was to persuade him to enter the farmyard and get him secured in a building.

John ordered me to stay behind him as we both closed on the bull. He certainly didn't like the idea of John approaching him and even less the idea of going somewhere he didn't want to go. John continued to shout and wave his pitchfork at him in an attempt to turn him towards the farm gate. He wasn't having any of it. His defiance was emphasised by his head lowering towards the ground, continually bellowing and snorting, his two big horns making patterns in the mist and his prancing action warning us not to go nearer to him. John was undeterred and moved closer to him. John ordered me to stay behind him. I didn't hesitate. I stayed five yards behind him, wondering how we could coax this ferocious-looking and -sounding bull back under control. John continued with his efforts to persuade the bull to turn towards the gate, but he wasn't having any of it.

Suddenly and as if there had been an explosion it happened. John ran out of patience and hurled his pitchfork at the bull. He completely missed him. This had no effect on getting him to turn towards the farm buildings, but seemed to give him the confidence to attack John. The attack was swift and decisive. Before John could move a yard the bull had scooped him off his feet and started to pound him into the ground. I can see that attack as if it was only yesterday, and I remember all my bodily sensations momentarily leaving me. The bull folded his front legs under his body and threw himself at John in an attempt to crush him. The bull's actions were reminiscent of the farm cat as she delivered her final actions before completing the kill of her latest mouse. With her front legs she would leap into the air and pounce on her doomed prey. In the same way the bull had John pinned to the ground. He was unable to get to his feet. The crushing action was sickening to watch and the speed of the bull's delivery left me in no doubt that this was going to be a fight to the death. It was so sudden, and at this point I hadn't moved. John was shouting at the bull as he twisted and lashed out with his fists to get him away from him. Now I closed in near to the bull to help John.

Then he shouted for help: "COLIN, HELP ME. DON'T LEAVE ME." That haunting shout for help was ringing in my ears. It was a cry of desperation. It isn't easy to explain that feeling.

John was fighting for his life, and now he had fallen silent. He was a couple of yards away from me, but the bull's body was obscuring him from my view. Somewhere beneath that heaving mass of steaming animal flesh John was fighting for his life. Everything was happening so quickly, but I was conscious that I had continued to move closer to the bull. My screams had no effect, but now I was in striking distance of the bull's head and in one movement I launched myself into this deadly combat swinging my leading pole, but John's silence made me fear the worst.

Engaging with Death

I crashed two quick and sickening blows on to his horns. They connected with him but seemed to bounce off him. The only effect they had was that he lifted his head slightly as if he was preparing to charge at me. My eyes filled with tears, stuck in a permanent staring state, unable to blink, unable to think of anything except continuing my assault. If I didn't get his head up and off John he would never get to his feet. John was shouting at the bull again, which encouraged me to maintain my ferocious attack on the bull. A voice in my head kept telling me to attack his face, deliver upper cuts to the lower jaw. I made the switch immediately. Two jaw-crushing blows landed on his face, then another. He was slowly responding, but his reactions were reminiscent of a world-champion heavyweight boxer who had mastered the art of seeing incoming blows and effortlessly changing his body's position so that punches just rolled off his body. Only the swiftest of blows were getting anywhere near to the bull's face. Throughout my attack I was also conscious that I was trying to prepare myself for the bull's counter-attack. I was no more than a yard in front of him. One leap and I would be grappling with death. Surely he would charge and in the blink of an eye sweep me off my feet, just as he had done to John. I was still screaming and maintaining my assault with crunching blows across his eyes.

John started to move. Could it be that he would be able to stand? In another split second he was crawling on his hands and knees away from the bull, then in a rolling motion he slowly got to his feet. I kept up my relentless and cruel attack with sickening blows to the bull's face. All this had taken place in split seconds. I continued to crash more blows into the bull's face. He was still only a yard away from me. His hot breath enveloped my body. I could taste it. And the voice in my head kept repeating the first message. Like a demented person I was using all my strength to smash the pole with sickening blows across his face. Once John had called for help I wasn't holding back, but I only succeeded in getting the bull to stand on his front legs, placing his horns and face closer to me. Would he lose interest in John and direct his attack on me? I had seen John getting swept off his feet, and once on the ground he was at the mercy of the bull. But I had to get the bull to stand and give space for John to lift his body from the ground. John had started to move. Dare I hope he could run? Yes. John started to stand and in one continuous movement he was running towards the gate.

"Colin, I'm all right. run for the gate." Then, more urgently as he got nearer to the gate and safety: "Run for the gate now."

But I stood locked in combat with death on four legs and couldn't immediately stop my attack just in case the bull took it to mean that he could sweep me to one side and relaunch the same deadly attack against me that he had done against John. Several more blows to the bull's face kept him standing, still facing me, about a yard away. I was alone, face-to-face and within touching distance of a steaming, growling, terrifyingly fast and dangerous bull, whose sole aim seemed to bring death and destruction to anything or anyone who got in his way.

Once John had run about fifteen yards he turned and shouted to me. This time his shout had an urgency and was more of an order and also threatening. The no-nonsense tone in his voice wasn't something I had witnessed previously. "Colin, run for the gate *now*." The emphasis on the last word was said in such a no-nonsense tone it was clear he wouldn't brook any dissent.

It wasn't a time to hesitate. I spun around and went into a sprint for the gate. I was much younger, slimmer and more agile than John, but what I previously witnessed had left me in no doubt that getting to the gate and securing safety wasn't going to be an easy task.

Running for Life

I looked up as I started running and could see John with his heavy frame draped over the top bar of the gate. He had closed the gate and was carefully watching for the bull's next move. He continued to call out to me. Now he was encouraging me to run as fast I could. That distance to the gate didn't seem to get any shorter. I wasn't able to look behind; my eyes were fixed on the top bar of the gate. John kept shouting encouragement. I summoned every ounce of effort to get to the gate. I couldn't hear the bounding gallop or the heavy snorting of the bull. I weighed up the gate, and at a full sprint tried to vault over the top bar. John had stood away from the gate to give me a clear view. I slithered and rolled over the top bar and crashed to the ground on the opposite side. I had made it. I was lying at John's feet, then felt the presence of his warm outstretched hand to help me to my feet. He held me in his arms in a bear hug as I tried to stand on my now 'jelly' legs, as I assured him I was uninjured. Beyond that I couldn't speak. We didn't need to. We looked at each other. Momentarily my face was a couple of inches away from his. I couldn't believe we were safe, but we were.

As John was lifting me in his arms I looked across at the bull. He was still pounding and punching the ground with his knees and crashing on John's cap, which had fallen off during the combat. He was completely out of control, totally unpredictable and a danger to everyone. Why hadn't the bull charged me before John's arrival at the field? One pounce and it would have been over and John would have met a completely different scene.

Lassie Saves Two Lives

As John was pulling me up from the ground, my eyes rolled everywhere. I glanced along the hedgerow to a clump of elderberry trees, which were inside the farmyard fence. They were about fifty yards away. Without my realising it, Lassie, my shadow, had never left me. So that was the answer to why the bull hadn't charged at me. She had remained immediately behind me throughout, even though I had been screaming at the top of my voice. I should have known she was at my heels, never far away from my side and always at the ready to reign in any errant farm animals. Her normal position would have been with her front legs bent and her breast touching the ground, rear legs straight and ready to create maximum thrust should I have given her the command to move in. She would have fixed her stare on the bull. Her jaw would have been open sufficiently to allow her tongue to spill out of her mouth, which even for this bull would have been a frightening sight and one challenge he wouldn't dare to rise to. She was looking at me as I was lying on the ground. She hesitated momentarily and, totally motionless, looked at me. Once she had satisfied herself that I was getting to my feet she disappeared from view to the quiet backwater of the farmyard. But you can be sure she would have heard my call should I have needed her again. This loyal servant had been waiting for my command to deal with the bull, but her presence had been enough to stop the fatal charge. That day she saved two lives, but we were too busy to fuss over her as we were still in a dangerous situation.

Just as John had earlier arrived at the broken farm gate, Tiger now arrived in the farmyard driving a tractor. His arrival gave us additional options to deal with this bull. John was obviously shaken. Then, totally out of character, he instructed Tiger to bring his shotgun to him from the Hall. No one spoke. Tiger had shut down the tractor's engine and the three of us now stood facing each other in total silence, desperately searching for something sensible to say. Surely he couldn't mean it. Tiger knew that he had meant it, but refused to obey. They stood eye to eye. I had never seen anyone defy John and wondered what he would do next. Over the years we had all accepted one of John's philosophies that he who pays the piper calls the tune. His management style was to allow opinions to get expressed, but once he stepped in and determined courses of action no further debate was allowed. This refusal was fighting talk, but thankfully John quickly regained his composure and realised he was acting out of all reason and character. He accepted Tiger's advice and prepared to return to his car, which was still on the grass verge alongside the A54. Tiger and I discussed how we would return the bull to the cowshed.

Whilst we were discussing our next move I could see John was continually clutching his ribs. He was confined to bed for several weeks after this event, but we never returned to this incident in our future conversations. Before leaving the farm for the day Lassie and the farm cat were in their usual place waiting outside the dairy, where they expected and always received a cup of milk in their feeding bowls. Lassie appeared none the worse for her experience.

The experience kept repeating in my mind – so much so that I couldn't recall what Mother had given me for my midday meal and sleep that night became illusive, but this wasn't a subject I would be discussing at home.

Inquest in the Cowshed

My usual practice was to start my day in the cowshed, where two other workers would be milking sixty cows. They stopped working and wanted a blow-by-blow account of the previous day's incident. After I had finished they were adamant that my actions had saved John from serious injury or even saved his life. My account to them highlighted John's unselfish and brave actions. I wanted them to realise that John initially took charge and stepped between me and the bull. He didn't have any need to get out of his car and wade out across a muddy field, but in doing so he had actually saved my life. They didn't agree, but concluded that we had both been fortunate to escape. Fate must have decreed that John was to drive past that field at the relevant time, but it did mean that both John and I were to survive. They agreed that Lassie crouched on the ground behind me was a contest too far for the bull, and this accounted for his failure to attack me. The bull was to be kept chained to his stall until John decided his fate.

JC Dies

John always announced his presence on the farm by calling out in his distinctively high-pitched voice. One day he wasn't expected, but when I went to see him I could see that he was in a sombre mood. He was clearly upset. He told me Mother had phoned him and he wanted to be the person to give me the bad news. Furthermore he wouldn't hear of me cycling home as he had made himself available for the day so that he could take me home, then to the hospital. It was a sad time. JC had finally succumbed to TB.

John Lea's relationship with his staff may have been delivered from a bale of hay or straw, but he carefully managed all his staff so that they all felt equal and all had an opinion that was worthy of consideration. This must have been a difficult time for John as the birth of his fifth child was imminent. We didn't have any worthwhile conversation on our journey to the hospital, but in an attempt to bring some level of realism to the whole episode he did comment that as one leaves this world another one joins it. His belief in his staff was exceptional. They were very important to him, and this was demonstrated by the way he cared for Mother and myself at the time of our family crisis.

Post-Office Robbery

Sometime later, when Lassie and I were bringing the herd in for milking, I saw a red post-office van parked partially hidden behind tall hedges. After my initial search around the van I reported it to John. It was an opportunity he couldn't miss. I was instructed to call at the police station on my way home and give a statement to the police. The next morning he was standing in the farmyard to seek confirmation that I had made the visit. My reception at the station wasn't what I expected. The Constable was most welcoming, which immediately dispelled my previously held opinions. John stressed his advice about the likelihood of a future career and I agreed to keep considering it. Although I didn't recognise it at the time, he was determined to see the police as my future career. His belief wouldn't be shaken.

Ron Bostock, Dairy-Herd Manager and Best Mate

In a conversation with me, John mentioned that he was about to engage another worker at the Hall – one he said that I would know. He didn't let the intrigue last for long and revealed that this new worker would be my old neighbour Ron Bostock. He was a natural dairy herdsman and after working for several years in the company of Tiger was to acquire many of his animal-husbandry skills, which he put to good use. His sense of quiet humour and ability to get on with the job made him a valuable member of the team.

One day Ron and I decided to answer an advert for two experienced herdsmen to manage a large dairy herd. We were both leaving a team of workers from whom we had gained a great deal of valuable experience and human social skills. These were only available from daily contact in often trying working conditions which required each team member to feel confident that their colleagues had the skills, experience and trust to place total reliance on their abilities. This degree of social intimacy formed the hub from which radiated close working relationships that spilled into the everyday management of John's herds of dairy cows and daily sustained a high level of morale amongst this very diverse workforce of nine men. John was extremely considerate towards us. He supported our initiative although he was losing two members of staff. He insisted that we should both return to him if our new venture didn't succeed. It was a difficult time, but Ron and I had felt this was the time to move on. To have John's support was extremely reassuring. We all shared many memories and in the process had become close working colleagues. With firm handshakes and knowing glances our new adventure had begun.

In 1959 we both moved to Sevenoaks, Kent, and took charge of a large dairy herd. We quickly got acquainted with the 'ladies' in a herd comprising mothers and many of their offspring. We had suddenly acquired a very large family, and whilst we never were touched with the foot-and-mouth plague it was easy to understand the trauma farmers endure in such circumstances. The herd responded to our gentle and persuasive management styles, maybe partly due to the owner and her mother who had previously been very hands-on and regarded the herd as their babies. We needed to quickly get them to respond to our individual styles as the pastures were widely spread across several large fields, and this was made the more urgent as we didn't have a farm dog. Nevertheless the task of bringing the herd into the milking sheds at 5 a.m. each morning never became an arduous task. They quickly responded to my first call, allowing me to walk into the advancing lines of swishing tails and nodding heads at the front of a large body that swayed in tune with their slow but deliberate gait. But it was more than that. At 5 a.m. the countryside was very much asleep. The absence of flies pestering our 'ladies' was noticeable, allowing them to give their full attention to everything going on around them. The autumn and spring early morning round-ups were often amidst a swirling mist which lay motionless across the meadows until as if by an invisible hand it parted to reveal the advancing herd. This was the time to visually inspect every cow. They responded as if I was invisible as I often felt the nudge of a huge damp nose reminding me to get out of their path as I threatened their position in the advancing lines closing in on the farmyard entrance gates.

To many, scenes like this will only ever be experienced on photographs, which reflects the magnitude of the losses we unconsciously incur as more people turn to living and working in conurbations. An outsider observing our milking sessions would probably have thought we had gone completely insane. Each of the animals had a pedigree and a name. Ron and I would be continually talking to individual cows, who would often raise their heads, chewing on food, and with their large eyes looking at us as if they understood every word that was being spoken. It wasn't surprising that our milk yields went through the roof and that the owner had a fit of depression twice a year when Ron and I returned home for a break. As we completed a three-year stint, Ron and I decided to return home and seek out fresh challenges.

Ron died in April 2012.

The author outside Buckingham Palace.

The author outside Brownley Road Police station, 1997.

The author and Inspector Vincent Alderman, prior to retirement with a combined service of sixty-five years, outside Brownley Road Police Station, 1997.

The author with BT community award.

A clock presented to the author on his retirement.

Rod Bamber, Arthur Watson, Lord Alf Morris and the author.

A police box at Stalybridge, 1964.

Dad's Helmet

Stalybridge, 1965
Cheshire County
Before boundary change of 1974
when Stalybridge became Tameside.

The Home Watch bus.

A visit by Michael Howard, MP and Home Secretary, and Wythenshawe and South Manchester Police Command Team to Wythenshawe Home Watch Committee.

Constable Paul Taylor and Sergeant David Rowson receiving visitors on the Home Watch bus.

Home Watch bus, 1994. Mike Satterthwaite, chairman of the Home Watch Committee (in the middle), Police Community Support Officers, and Constables Paul Taylor and Helen Lunn.

Home Watch bus en route to Woodhouse Park carnival.

Making a start on Fairywell pond, the author, director of Nymex and two local residents.

David Hilton, on the left, supervising local residents during the early stages of creating steps and paths at Fairywell.

David Hilton at Fairywell.

The probation service making a difference at Fairywell.

Fairywell nearing completion.

BT community award for Fairywell Nature Park.

Ray Hulston, Home Watch, assisting the police on an open day in Fairywell Nature Park.

Fairywell open day.

Carnival time at Woodhouse Park, Wythenshawe.

Scouts 'bag packing' in a supermarket.

Well done! At Base Wythenshawe Hospital, the author, Brian and Glynn.

Medals.

Remembrance plaque.

Lassie, our farm dog, 1952–1957.

CHAPTER 5

POUNDING THE BEAT, 1962

During November 1961 my initial application to join the Cheshire Constabulary was followed by a home visit by a senior officer. My lunchtime interview was around the fireside. My brother Allan was present as, unusually for him, he had taken a day off work with a head cold. The interview was extremely friendly; both our journeys to serve the community had begun.

On 26 February 1962 I boarded the Middlewich-to-Northwich bus clutching a small suitcase, glad to jump on board to get out of the raging blizzard – and so began my journey into the police service. Watching the countryside scene through the bus window, I was conscious that managing those intensely loyal and trusting dairy cows would now be confined to the past. It was sad, but life had to move on. Ultimately I found myself sat in front of large wooden desk, behind which was seated the Chief Constable. He was in uniform and appeared very serious, and I wasn't about to engage in any lengthy conversation with him. For some reason of all the interviews conducted whilst in the police service this is one that I clearly remember. He told me that he had already accepted three other candidates that morning. He emphasised that my educational record since leaving school had left much to be desired and wouldn't stand comparison with the others', and he said he had doubts about my suitability. He concluded by saying he was confident the other three candidates could manage the intensity of the three-month Police Training Centre course, but could I? Suddenly my mouth opened and I said I expected to work harder to achieve the same results. He quickly pushed a form across the desk and told me to sign my name in the space provided. Then he said he was to give me some advice.

He said, "We carry out our duties with the consent of the public. You should consider your police career against your farming experiences and that you will only reap what you sow."

Within the hour I was at a local police station and magistrate's court swearing the oath of allegiance and being whisked in a black police van to Cheadle Hulme Police Station with a bundle containing my police uniform to attend another interview, this time with the divisional commander.

Hazel Grove (Bullock Smithy, 1754 – Hazel Grove, 1886)

The commander had a soft Irish accent. He emphasised the importance of my farming experience, which immediately won my attention, and concluded with advice that initially I wasn't to understand.

Looking across huge piles of paper files he said, "Never forget, Constable, sex is the most powerful thing known to man. it removes kings from crowns."

On meeting my sergeant at Hazel Grove, he took the time to explain the two pearls of wisdom I had received earlier that day. My career in the police initially seemed destined to be short-lived as I very nearly didn't make the first day. I had caught the 192 bus from my lodgings, which was to stop at the police station. The conductor forgot, but after my prompting he hurriedly stopped the bus a mile further away. I ran back to the police station just in time to attend the 6-a.m. parade, much to the amusement of the other two constables on duty. At that time the police station overlooked the main road and was the home station to about a dozen constables, one sergeant and one inspector. The Inspector and his family lived at the station.

Death of a Newspaper Schoolboy

Three months later I returned to the station after escaping from the training centre. I hadn't been at the station for more than a couple of weeks when I was thrown into my first big test. I was patrolling along the A6 during the morning when the driver of a car stopped and shouted that about a mile away towards Stockport he had seen a young boy lying on the edge of the road, which he believed was as a result of being hit by a car. In 1962 our communications relied on phones in police stations, so I stopped the next driver of a car going towards Stockport. A schoolboy was lying on the footpath and near to a newspaper shop. Several people had gathered around. The newsagent had alerted the ambulance and Stockport Borough Police, who were an independent police force until 1974. This young schoolboy had been struck by a car on the A6 and had died instantly. I examined the young boy, and in spite of my untrained eye I determined that he had died. I draped my cape over the young boy and waited for the Stockport Borough Police to arrive. Five minutes later a Stockport officer arrived on his bike. I thought my role had finished.

When I returned to my station, my sergeant wanted a full update, after which he instructed me to visit the boy's parents as they lived in Hazel Grove and pass on the information about the death of their son. I wasted no time, and shortly afterwards found myself standing on the footpath at the end of the driveway leading to the deceased boy's home. This wasn't going to be easy. I had seen my mother react to the news of death in the family and recalled her insistence that the whole house would be thrown into darkness and that no one should speak above a whisper and only in a sombre tone. More importantly, she would always visit neighbours and offer her support. I stood looking at the house. I had to move. No one was around. The driveway had toys strewn on it, as did the one next door. It wasn't more than twenty yards in length, but to me it seemed to go on for miles. Obviously there were other young children at both houses. Just as I was about to step on to the drive I felt the urge to spin quickly and I found myself walking down the neighbouring drive.

A young woman answered the door – obviously the mother as she half turned and shouted to her children to make less noise before turning to me with an enquiring look and waited for me to speak. We remained standing at the front door and I remember asking if she would help me with this problem. Her reaction to the information I gave her was immediate. She clasped her face in her hands and quietly sobbed. A young face appeared around the living-room door. No other noise was made. It was as if her children had sensed, if not partly heard, the terrible news about the accident concerning their neighbour and playmate. What seemed to be several minutes later, but was less, she took her hands away from her face and shouted to the children to stay inside the house as she would only be next door and would be back home shortly. She turned to me. She was now in complete control. I was instructed to follow her to her neighbour's front door.

The two young mothers held each other in their arms, crying uncontrollably for several minutes. Children in this house were momentarily bewildered, but their neighbour gave them instructions to wait in their living room as we gathered together and whispered in the hallway. The death message had been delivered.

What prompted me to firstly go to the neighbour's for assistance will always remain a mystery, but it was obviously the right thing to do. My sergeant was satisfied, but if this was policing perhaps I hadn't made a wise choice as the faces of these two young mums were difficult to get out of my mind, to say nothing about the young schoolboy crumpled lifeless on the footpath alongside a busy main road. At this time I would have much preferred to be calling home that herd of dairy cows and watching them slowly emerge from the early morning mist, in single file, swaying gently from side to side with full udders, watching me with their large honest eyes. But that was now a different world and I had to get on with this one, where protecting people had become my priority. In any case, police management at this particular station allowed officers freedom to develop their skills; and whilst I learnt later that this wasn't necessarily a universal quality throughout the police service, at this station for the moment it was a happy place to be.

Pub Brawl

Hazel Grove developed partly because of its close proximity to Manchester, stagecoach transport links, coal mining and silk mills. Supporting the local population was a myriad of public houses.

One evening local youths congregating in the Grove Inn decided to let their beer get the better of them. The Sergeant summoned me to the station and filled me in as we went to see the licensee. I asked if he wanted to run the half-mile, but he told me to keep with him and that any extra time it took us to get to the pub would serve to allow the fighting youths to 'beat the hell out of each other'. I thought that was exactly what we were trying to prevent, but the Sergeant was leading the charge. Getting to the front door, I was instructed to stay behind him. This was the second time I had been instructed to stay out of the firing line; but instead of a young demented bull, this time it was a gang of about eighteen young men engaged in a brawl. Several groups were fighting in the main room. Tables were lying on their sides, beer glasses strewn across the floor. Voices were raised and as I stood trying to take in every detail of the scene I could see the licensee was hiding behind the bar. It resembled a scene from the Wild West, but the Sergeant strode forward and into the room. My right hand was nestling on the top of my truncheon and the other was holding the handcuffs securely in place – both of which I would use as weapons in an emergency to restore the peace. As if by magic, the Sergeant's arrival brought a total hush to the bar area, all the youths turned to face us, some started to square up to us as if in preparation for the fight to follow.

Then the Sergeant shouted to all to announce our presence. He held both hands up to about shoulder height, addressed all the youths and shouted, "You may knock us down, but others will follow."

As we were the only two police officers on duty and stood in this uneasy, tense face-to-face situation I knew we were on our own. But they didn't.

I didn't have to wait long for the Sergeant to address the youths again. He set out his ground rules, and gave the youths a way out without further police action. His maturity was such that he convinced the youths who were hell-bent on smashing tables and chairs around our bodies that we were not invincible and were prepared to negotiate, but as a last resort he wouldn't stand any nonsense and would call upon reinforcements if necessary. He told them the licensee wouldn't be pursuing any action regarding the spilt beer or broken glasses, but this was their last chance to disperse and go home. To my amazement, like lambs they filed out of the front door. The licensee, who was still behind the bar, became more confident, stood up and was overcome with relief, completely delighted, and apologised profusely to the Sergeant. I had just witnessed the actions of an experience officer, a Second World War veteran and a brave man.

Meeting Barbara

During one Sunday lunchtime traffic was extremely light. Boredom was beginning to take over and I was heading back to the station, looking forward to finishing my shift. Suddenly a motorcycle engine came roaring down the A6 towards me. Number One Stop Signal was executed and I stood in the middle of the approaching motorcycle's lane. It was an old small bike that seemed to make more noise than speed, but I caused the rider to stop anyway. There was absolutely nothing out of place and everything worked. The rider was later to produce driving documents.

As I entered the station the office man stated that the documents were in order and asked if there was any reason to retain details from this young lady. I said I had no recollection of speaking to any young lady. The office man soon corrected me and revealed that the motorcyclist under the helmet was a young lady.

A couple of days later my shift partner, who was courting a local young lady, told me he had arranged for Barbara and his girlfriend to accompany us and we were to spend the afternoon driving around the Peak District, which is on the doorstep of Hazel Grove. Of all the lucky days I was to have, this was the luckiest. It actually got even better when I was to meet an exceptionally pleasant, caring and considerate person – her mother.

The following weekend L-plates were placed on my car and Barbara for the first time got behind the steering wheel of my car and drove the thirty-plus miles to Middlewich. Later, in 1964, we married and moved into a police house in Stalybridge.

Capers Crossing the Road

Escorting schoolchildren across the busy A6 was an essential duty for police officers in the sixties. It would be difficult to imagine how a police officer could inject humour into this role, but how mistaken can you be! I was in the police station when the office man called me to the station window, which overlooked the A6. One of our colleagues was shepherding children across the road and he had decided to rewrite the rules. This was also the age when police officers wore capes – the sight greeting my eyes was the officer dressed in his cape over his uniform, walking in a crouched position, cape now dragging along the road whilst he was talking to the children face-to-face. Outwardly it appeared the officer was only as tall as the primary-school children. Just how the vehicle drivers coped with this humorous situation I will leave to the reader to imagine, but the station officer thought it an outstanding feat and the children loved it.

Runaway Horse and Cart

It was during one afternoon that I was doing the same duty, but at the opposite end of the village. Fifty yards away from a set of automatic traffic lights was the location of the school crossing patrol. Several groups of children had already left the school and had passed over the road, and several more were congregating waiting for me to stop the traffic. At this point I realised that a rag-and-bone man's horse and cart were trotting along the A6 towards my position. I looked again and realised that the rag-and-bone man wasn't with the horse and the horse was now galloping at full speed towards me. I shouted to the children to remain at the back of the footpath and not to move. They couldn't see the danger, but they obeyed my shouts and kept away from the edge of the road. The horse and cart had now galloped through the traffic lights; I could see the cart was piled with old rags. This rag-and-bone man was a common sight to me as Hazel Grove was on his regular collecting route. The name of the owner was printed on the side of the cart and he was a well-known local person. He always acknowledged me with a raised hand or gave a knowing nod of his head as he sat on the shafts nearest to the body of the cart. What could have happened to him? I moved into the centre of the road to see if I could get a better view of the person in charge, but my worst fears were now being realised. The horse was at full gallop, unescorted and coming straight towards me. The A6 traffic lights at Torkington Road were showing red against the oncoming horse and cart. The pace didn't slacken as the horse continued at full gallop, but now he was heading towards me without the presence of any following traffic as they were held at the lights. The first driver to emerge from Torkington Road clearly saw the danger and stopped once he had got on to the A6. Traffic coming in the opposite direction picked up my stop signal, which brought oncoming traffic from the opposite direction to a standstill. I now had a gap of traffic-free road of about fifty yards as the horse and cart approached me. As no traffic had joined the A6 from Torkington Road a gap of another fifty yards had been created between my position and the back of a stationary double-decker bus. Where was Jim 'Tiger' Smith now? I moved to the horse's left side and called out to him. No response – no change in direction or speed either. I continued to call out and shout to him.

I could hear Tiger shouting, "Get him to look at you with his ears. Show him he can trust you. Take control with a firm voice. Get hold of the bit. Hold on to him," ringing in my ears in his usual no-nonsense manner.

All manner of messages go racing through your mind when you are under this magnitude of pressure. I stood directly in the path of this out-of-control horse and cart, but I stood my ground. Something had to happen – the collision was only a few seconds away. Was I going to be half carried and dragged into the back of the stationary bus, or would the horse stumble and fall on to me, causing the cart to overturn and come to rest who knows where? Previously he had trotted along this route many times and instinctively knew he was on the way back to his stables. Now he was almost upon me, but I could see he had picked up my shouts. His head was held high, his reins were hanging loose on the nearside of the cart and he was still in full gallop. I knew he could see and hear me as the distance between us grew less and less. I had no idea where the children were. Imminent danger was staring me in the face. That was all I could hear or see. Both my arms were held high above my head as I continued to call out to the horse.

Then it happened: I turned to run in the same direction just at the time the horse's head impacted into my chest and the shiny buttons of my uniform. I needed to run as fast as I could to keep alongside. I tried to match the speed of his gallop, but realised I was losing ground and he was in fact dragging me along with him. We were locked together. My desperately held out right hand was trying to get a firm hold of his bridle. My hand caught hold of the leather strap at the top of his head, near to his ears, and from that moment I thought I was getting some measure of control, but this wasn't going to be easy as his head pushed into me and made my steps take leaps and bounds as if I was walking on the moon. In those split seconds I was holding my own. I was managing to keep free from his hooves although I didn't have any control over the direction we were going in. I had to run faster as he appeared unable to slow down fast enough for me. I was also afraid that his metal shoes would lose grip and he would slip and fall. Now my hand was firmly gripping the bit in the horse's mouth, but the rear of the still stationary double-decker bus was now looming closer and closer and stationary traffic on the opposite carriageway and positioned alongside the bus was effectively blocking the road at that point. For a few split seconds a collision seemed inevitable. My rubber-soled police boots were screaming at the road surface as I held his head into my chest. My legs and feet were acting as additional brakes, as if I was the anchorman on a tug-of-war rope to assist the effort the horse was making to stop before we collided with the back of the bus. The gallop became a canter, then immediately a trot. We were still standing. We stopped a couple of yards away from the bus. I don't know who was trembling and shaking more, the horse or myself.

Once the horse and cart had passed the usual assembly point for the children they must have crossed the road and continued their homeward journey as if nothing had happened.

I continued to hold the horse as I was afraid he might bolt again, but he was quickly settling down as I continued to verbally reassure him. As I stood holding the horse I was looking behind us to see if the rag-and-bone man was anywhere in sight. As I stood talking to the horse I felt two arms grasp me around the waist. I spun around and recognised the person as the rag-and-bone man. He collapsed into my arms as the incident had drained him to the point where he was almost a lifeless wreck. I moved the horse and cart to the roadside and encouraged the man to sit on the cart, in his normal position just behind the shafts and nearest to the kerb, and give me an account of what had happened. Something had spooked his horse – he thought it was the noise of a metal dustbin. The sudden surge of speed by his horse had caused him to lose his grip on the reins; he had overbalanced and slipped off the cart shafts. He realised as he picked himself up from the road that he wasn't going to catch him unless he slowed or stopped galloping. When he couldn't catch him, total panic had overcome him. He had feared the worst. He had been in charge of this horse for years and regularly collected rags from housing estates along the A6 in Hazel Grove. I could see that he was devoted to this horse and this incident had completely unnerved him.

After a few minutes he managed to stand again and as I left him he stood with both arms around the horse's head, visibly shaken and weeping uncontrollably. The whole incident had happened so quickly. Five minutes or so later he resumed his homeward journey. The schoolchildren had all gone home; my shift had finished. Instead of being embroiled in a scene of unbridled carnage, no one had been injured. The job was done – job finished.

'All's well that ends well,' I thought, but how wrong can you be?

Invoking the Wrath of the Chief Inspector

About a week after the runaway-horse incident a chief inspector's inspection of six probationary constables was to take place at Hazel Grove Police Station. As this was my home station I arrived early. These inspections were difficult to predict, firstly as the inspecting officer was unknown to any of the other constables, and secondly as the subject we were to be tested on was known only to the inspecting officer. As soon as I walked through the front door of the station I stood in shock horror. An old bike had been left on the stairs and half a dozen other items of property were strewn around between the front door and the upstairs inspection meeting room. I couldn't understand why any of these items were cluttering up the station or why the office man hadn't seen them. Quickly I removed all of them to the property store, then visited the inspection meeting room to wait for the others to arrive.

The Chief Inspector was sat behind the desk and we sat in silence until everyone was seated. The topic selected was 'Awareness and Observations'. Everyone was asked to describe their route and any unusual items they had seen between the front door and the meeting room. The first officer quickly concluded his account as he had very little to say. At this point I realised I had ruined the lecture, so I interrupted and explained my actions to the Chief Inspector. If he was amused he didn't show it, and he quickly selected another subject, which was 'Completing Pocket Notebooks'.

Failing to Submit an Incident Report

This change of subject didn't concern me as my sergeant was keen to ensure that I complied with all the force rules. As each officer had undergone the required scrutiny they were allowed to return to their home stations; I was the last to have my book examined. The Chief Inspector carefully flicked through each page of my notebook. Was he going to say anything about wrecking his lecture?

I didn't have to wait long before he came across two lines in my book which read, 'Stopped runaway horse and cart on London Road.' He stared at it for several seconds, then needed to know every detail. I hadn't discussed this with my sergeant as a discussion would take place when he carried out his periodic checks. Furthermore, I hadn't submitted any written report about the incident. This was turning out to be a nightmare. For one moment I thought both the Sergeant and I would be disciplined.

The Chief Inspector concluded the scrutiny by informing me he would be discussing this with my sergeant, but insisted on giving me some advice: "Constable don't hide your light under a bushel."

Later the Sergeant explained the meaning of this and stressed that whilst he would have preferred to have seen a written report, nevertheless the Chief Inspector had been satisfied with the ultimate outcome of the incident and, with the Sergeant, found my lecture-wrecking actions hilarious.

CHAPTER 6

STALYBRIDGE

A Town Stuck in Time

As I cycled to my new station a first-class view of the town could be seen from Stamford Street. As Stalybridge was nestling in a hollow on either side of the River Tame, with a canal constructed to accompany it in many places, it was easy to see why initially it had been a bustling mill town. The most striking feature was the housing estate on the rising ground on the far side of the town. It was early March. The weather was bitterly cold and the occupants of the estate were burning coal or other non-smokeless fuel, and a large plume of black smoke hung ominously over the town. What was this place? It certainly looked uninviting as years of smoke and grime had added to its character and, as I later discovered, had probably influenced a resident in a neighbouring village – Lowry. Bitterly cold wind deterred pedestrian shoppers, schoolchildren were still in school and the whole place had a foreboding, desolate feel to it. I didn't dwell on this, but continued to my new station and colleagues I had yet to meet.

Three Rooms in the Town Hall

The station was part of the town hall, which was showing the effects of continual smoke and traffic pollution. This was betrayed by windows that carried layers of grime deposited over many years. The police station comprised three offices, a small room that was the canteen, three cells, an interconnecting corridor that doubled as access to the magistrates' court and a parade area for uniformed constables. All the parading officers stood in a line side by side facing the Sergeant.

No Name, Just a Number

I was introduced to all the other constables, but wasn't yet to realise that my Christian name was being used for the last time. Dehumanisation had begun. From that moment on I became known only by my collar number (531). The irony of previously managing a large herd of dairy cows comprising mothers, daughters and sisters, and talking to them using their names, then joining an organisation unable to effectively communicate, wasn't lost on me. I recognised that this was a disciplined service, but during my first two years' service I had retained my individuality and this distancing from the supervisory officers was my first indication of an existence that was purposefully cultivated to treat constables with the same austerity and coldness that exuded from the cold black walls of the police station.

My first day was to be spent with another officer, who organised a relay of officers to visit the whole borough. It seemed like a walking marathon in a very hilly area. Five minutes after the appointed shift start time, ten constables would regularly march out of the police station escorted by their sergeant to their allotted beats for that shift. The town had direct-line communications by way of police boxes that resembled Dr Who's Tardis. Additionally the town had half a dozen street lights which had suspended from the top of them a green light which would only be illuminated when the office man wanted the beat officer to contact the station. This was prior to possessing personal radios. Failure to respond to this light within five minutes would be viewed as a disciplinary offence. Inside the police boxes was a small wooden bench on which stood a direct-line phone.

Two Tables and a Wonky Leg

Refreshments would be taken in the police station canteen. Everyone brought their own food and brewing tackle. The canteen contained two small tables. It had been arranged as a symbol of control and bullying by the last remnants of former borough police officers. One of the tables had a wonky leg – needless to mention, this was for the sole use of county officers. The other was for borough officers, who took great delight in visiting this room when a county officer was taking refreshments, but only to check on compliance with their instructions.

Fortunately my initial service during my first two years at Hazel Grove allowed me to stand back, privately question and watch the antics of some misguided officers, who were obviously influenced and some totally controlled by this inspector. My meetings with him on the beat were eye-opening. He was a total contradiction as he had developed different characteristics for different sections of the community and his officers. Any meeting in the town would constantly be interrupted by his acknowledgement of members of the community. They had a great deal of respect for him and he seemed to be known to everyone. This aspect of policing was very reassuring. We were their police and their support and encouragement was freely given, which made it all the more difficult to understand why any conversation with the public whilst walking the beat was totally frowned upon. But in this town residents and their families came first – a far cry from what I was to experience later in my career. Treatment and management of his staff was also a different matter. It had become well known amongst other members of the Cheshire Constabulary that officers were often asked to serve at Stalybridge because of some prior disciplinary action, or the officer was newly married or a new recruit. It was also equally well known that officers came and went as easily as walking through a revolving door. Oddly enough, this atmosphere only served to strengthen a feeling of camaraderie amongst many of the constables as they endured the hostilities of the half a dozen borough constables, and the excessive use of authority by sergeants who, similar to the Inspector, were impervious to any accountability and managed policing in this town like a dictatorship. This control was reinforced continuously.

Directing Traffic at Bowerfold

I was directed to perform duty at Stalybridge Celtic football team's home fixture. I escorted the Inspector to the ground and performed traffic duty until five minutes prior to kick-off. At that point I escorted him to the turnstiles. For one moment I thought I was to witness his human and emotional responses as we watched the game. I should have known better. As we approached the turnstiles to usher him into the ground he turned and gave instructions to resume foot patrol, visit and check on a dozen temporarily unoccupied houses in the borough as the occupants were probably on holiday. They had previously informed the station officer, who kept a record of these requests and all the visits carried out.

This aspect of policing served to frame my opinions about the limitations of foot patrols and the education of the public that everyone must look to take greater control of their lives and family responsibilities and not to rely on others, including the police, to fulfil socially based tasks. As there was never any intended social contact with residents when inspecting these properties, the full purpose of these police actions wasn't being realised.

After the match he would check my pocketbook to ensure that I had carried out the property inspections. The opportunity for local residents and many of the younger generation to share in a common bond in a simple matter such as supporting the town's football team, which had the scope to galvanise their support for the local bobby as one of them, had also been lost.

Time Expired

The magistrates' court was a connecting door away from the police station and cells. Usually time spent in court was in addition to the normal shift, and that time would be entered into the time-off book. After three months, any time remaining would be forfeited. The Inspector would take great delight in refusing any time off, then on his visits to the parades would relish the fact that he was frequently cancelling excess time on duty as time expired. Whilst this was totally unacceptable, all the sergeants were complicit in the system and all the constables accepted the futility of any challenges in the event of the threat of the Inspector's version of police discipline. The merger of Stalybridge Borough Police and the Cheshire Constabulary in 1947 just hadn't been accepted by this inspector, but the crime lay at the door of officers occupying higher ranks who had failed to exercise an acceptable level of accountability.

Where's the Body?

I only attended one incident with the Inspector. A local rubber-mouldings company had reported an accident in their factory, and using the police Morris Minor I drove the Inspector to the site. The manager was asked to identify the body of the worker who had been involved in the accident. He waved his arms and said he was all around. Further investigations showed the worker had fallen into a vat of rubber which was being processed from a solid to a fluid state. It was a gruesome scene and it was not easy to gather the body parts to try to make one whole body. The investigations were limited to one small area and a couple of workmen. We determined that death would have been instantaneous.

Indomitable Spirits in the Slums

Whilst the lot of the police was not a happy one, Stalybridge was inhabited by people who were welcoming, warm, hospitable and extremely supportive of their local police.

Living conditions on the Castle Hall housing estate were directly out of a previous century. Originally the terraced houses were built by mill owners. Previously the area had been known as 'Paradise' as the gentle slopes were liberally covered by trees and pastures. What resulted was too awful to contemplate. Half a dozen houses shared a communal washing area and shared one toilet, which the occupants emptied. Single houses comprised one ground-floor room connected by a stairway to an upper room. These warrens of houses were connected by cobbled streets. Each house seemed to have an iron grating beneath the living-room window. It gave direct access to the cellar, and coal was poured into the cavern on a regular basis. Everyone knew each other. Disease was rife. Public houses stood on almost every corner. Flagstones inside the houses were scrubbed with donkey stones (a form of white concrete produced in slabs) and a sign of affluence was a rag carpet pegged by the occupants. Everyone was in the same boat – they all worked together trying to exist or improve their lot.

In this situation I felt extremely privileged. I could witness their daily hardship yet not be a part of it. I couldn't help feeling that here powerful reasons existed why we as a nation had been victorious in two world wars. There were daily examples of community cohesion and collective caring in which face-to-face contact dominated. The community's resilience and determination to survive were inspirational, and made my time at Stalybridge a memorable one.

Barbara Gives Birth to Sandra

In June 1965 Barbara gave birth to our daughter Sandra. It was a Monday. I had taken Barbara to Tameside Hospital during the night and as I finished giving evidence in the magistrates' court the following morning I was given the concession to phone the hospital and check on Barbara's condition. She was just about to give birth to our daughter Sandra. Our family life at Stalybridge was a very happy time, but we moved out of our police house and into our own home in 1971.

'It's a Long Way to Tipperary' (Jack Judge)

The town centre was a compact area of shops, including the Co-op and Woolworth's. Finding an insecure front door to a building one day, I decided to explore further. As I gently pushed the door open the smell of decay hit me. The whole town suffered from the same disease, so it wasn't anything that unusual. I moved very slowly, checking the upper parts of the building to make sure I wasn't in danger of being crushed by any falling pieces of masonry. A couple of pigeons fluttered somewhere inside the building. It was eerie and difficult to make out shapes, but after several seconds of standing motionless inside the front door I had to hesitate because I couldn't quite believe what I was seeing. It was like stepping into another world. I had walked into a disused theatre (the Hippodrome). A stage overlooked the stalls, which comprised many rows of red velvet seats, and along the sides were what appeared to be private boxes. Curtains still hung at each side of the stage. I still hadn't moved. Unusual noises added to the atmosphere and by this time I could feel the goose pimples bulging all over my body. 'Could it be haunted?' was a thought that flashed through my brain, but I quickly dismissed it. No, I couldn't hear faint refrains of now long-gone artistes, but the noise bringing me quickly back to the present was a couple of rats scurrying across the stage.

Some daylight had pierced the interior through dislodged roof tiles, and as I retreated to the daylight I could only think of the importance of these places. The Hippodrome had given local artistes the opportunity to develop their skills to provide entertainment and enjoyment. It was a place for gossiping with friends and renewing old contacts, allowing the local inhabitants to drift in and relax after toiling in health-damaging and dangerous working conditions after what must have seemed like endless hours in local mills, foundries and the light industries that these resourceful people had developed to maintain their livelihoods and communities. Many of the people in these audiences would meet again in their local churches and chapels, which seemed to compete for popularity with the public houses, but they all combined to improve quality of life, the importance of which seems to have slipped off our radar screens in our haste to make the best of our lives within a world increasingly intent on reducing the need to remain gregarious. Now it was just another building amongst many in this town that was in the process of being demolished.

Opposite this theatre is a public house with a plaque showing an inscription to mark the work of Jack Judge, who in 1911 and allegedly for a bet of two shillings and sixpence wrote and completed in one day the song 'It's a Long Way to Tipperary'. This was popularised during the First World War.

What was probably not fully realised is that it wasn't just

buildings that were being demolished; it was the remnants of communities, their lifestyles, habits and pleasure pursuits, which we were to witness again in those mining villages during a long-drawn-out and bitter dispute with the government of the day. Eventually, and in the face of public dissent, it would crumble and perish against an unstoppable oncoming tide of change.

Rod Laver v Ken Rosewall

Almost opposite the derelict theatre was the gents' outfitters' shop run by Jack Coggan. His family had run the business for several generations and he was also managing the town's indoor tennis stadium. I had no sooner started my afternoon shift than Jack ran into the street to give me a briefing about the event to be held that evening in his stadium. He had secured the attendance of Rod Laver and Ken Rosewall, who were to give an exhibition tennis match. Having these two tennis legends in Stalybridge was mind-blowing, but Jack wanted my assurance that we would work together to make the event a success. Initially I was delighted; then I thought about the undesirable elements that the event would attract as the town could quickly become infested with car thieves and I was the only officer on duty in the town centre.

He also hatched a plot that would get me into the stadium to watch the game. Five minutes before the start Jack dragged me off the streets to the reception area, which overlooked the courts, on the premise that several youths were looking to create a disturbance. I stood with him and agreed I would stay to see the legends start their knock-up before the event. Everything was going to plan. All those attending were seated and there was an atmosphere of excitement and expectancy. A thrilling game was about to commence.

Mistaken Identity?

Four late arrivals – two couples – hurriedly entered the reception area. Three quickly walked to their seats, but the fourth hesitated and let out a loud scream. She made a direct lunge at Jack Coggan and me, but as she got closer we realised she was shouting at me.

"It's so lovely to see you again. What are you doing here?"

Before I could regain any composure, she had seen her party disappear towards the seating area and with an apologetic wave of her arms she also disappeared.

Jack had taken great delight in witnessing my embarrassment and wasn't going to allow it to pass without more investigation. He was revelling in my inability to give him a satisfactory answer. I was totally confused. She must have mistaken me for someone else. I protested to Jack that she must be mistaken, but he wasn't accepting any of my protestations. We finally agreed to disagree. He didn't believe me and it remained that way until I came to write these lifetime recollections. Her sudden appearance and yells of recognition accompanied by the urgency of her approach as she erupted with arms waving completely threw me off balance as I was mentally fixed on policing this sporting event. Initially I was concerned about my own safety. Was she going to stop before crashing into me? She was walking quickly and straight at me.

I had no reason to recall this incident until I was writing these recollections. Then as the lines appeared across these pages the face and name eluded me no more. She was that young schoolgirl, now a sophisticated young lady, who was half dragged by the proprietress of the dancing school to where I was sitting to be introduced as my new dancing partner. Our social skills were so undeveloped that I think we danced together for several weeks before we both realised we were allowed to talk. We did improve sufficiently to fulfil the proprietress's belief that I would manage to circumnavigate the dance floor without crippling my partner or knocking anyone to the floor, and the speed at which she approached me all those many years later at the tennis tournament is a testament to the proprietress's belief and my partner's courage.

My move to Sevenoaks in 1959 with Ron Bostock took me away from mid Cheshire, but three years later I had joined the Cheshire Constabulary.

This town of ginnels and gaggles (narrow restricted pathways usually giving access along very step terrains) and decaying property, serviced by trolleybuses, nevertheless had its own individual charm. Pounding the beat in the dead of night always struck me as a useless exercise, with only rats (the four-legged types), a sergeant who I suspected was equally unimpressed with this policing system, and the danger of flying roof slates which had become dislodged over time in previous high winds. Walking the beat became an exercise in survival against the chatter and song of the fast-moving River Tame flowing beneath the bridges in the town, and our policing activities were marooned in a previous century.

Like the blood coursing through our veins, there was a general constancy of the engaging nature of the majority of the town's inhabitants. Shopkeepers would acknowledge my presence as I walked the beat, and local people walking in the town would step into the road if they thought space on the footpath was too limited for us to pass side by side. The Inspector would raise his cap to anyone who approached him. His knowledge of local people had been developed over almost forty years, but it was to be a fast-disappearing world where human contact, social interactions and the ownership of 'our police' would slowly give rise to the blight of unfettered, unchallenged and emerging undesirable elements, with debilitating infectious habits (alcohol and drugs) that would now compare poorly with yesteryear's poverty-ridden communities.

Fighting at the Bus Station

I witnessed further evidence of the Inspector's knowledge of local people after I arrested two youths in the bus station for causing a disturbance. Often in the late evening the bus station would be a gathering place for local youths. On this occasion two youths refused to behave and I arrested them. Getting them to the police station was fraught with difficulties as a flight of about forty steps had to be overcome before the police station entrance could be gained. On each side of the steps were handrails, which the two youths grabbed hold of, making my progress very difficult. Just before I was about to give up, the borough constable on duty in the office appeared and rescued the situation. He was a man of huge proportions and tremendous strength, and we made short work of carrying both youths into the station.

Tremendously relieved, I followed to find the Inspector was stood confronting them both. The youths had immediately fallen to their knees and begged his forgiveness. For the next five minutes he questioned both youths as they lay on the floor – not about the incident, but about their parents and family. I stood amazed witnessing this conversation, which allowed the Inspector to demonstrate his intimate knowledge of their family and their history. Whilst I was in awe of his prowess, I knew his character was seriously flawed as he continually demonstrated his impervious and scant regard for the views of others to achieve his own slanted opinions irrespective of the hardships they might cause.

Three weeks later the youths would appear before him in the magistrates' court, where summary justice comprised a fine of two weeks wages for each youth. The court was in the town hall adjacent to the rooms occupied by the police. The Inspector would present cases and all the evidence to the magistrates and they would dispense justice. There was almost a family atmosphere about these courtroom sessions – they had a localism that was destroyed by the creation of the Crown Prosecution Service, which also seemed to hasten the popularity of custodial sentencing. Others have commented on the effects that poverty and hard work can achieve to shape the characters within the community and the influences they can bring on others, such as the following.

Streets away from Paradise, by Eli Hague (Reminiscences of Stalybridge)

I feel Eli Hague's comment concisely captures the spirit and values that describe the local inhabitants of Stalybridge and the effect that their daily lives had on me and others.

> Throughout the long years that have elapsed my mind has returned more and more to that little community of mills and factories, cobbled streets and warm hearted folk who, without realising it, first instilled in me the moral values and aspirations which have ever since guided and sustained me.

This reminds me of Barbara's shopping excursions in Stalybridge. At this time she would have Sandra in the pram. As she visited specific shops the pram had to be positioned to allow Sandra to see what was going on; otherwise the whole town became aware of her presence. Disruption didn't end there. Every uniformed police officer encountered in the town centre was instantly identified as 'Daddy', followed by a short conversation. Perhaps at this tender age this was Sandra's way of seeking attention. She hasn't changed.

As a police officer, my mind searched for answers to stop the moral decay in values within our communities and to discover what was likely to fill the void. In Chapter 12 I describe how our efforts to spread the gossip and gospel of parish policing went some way towards furthering these aims and the thoughts of Eli Hague.

Amongst all the rubble of partly demolished buildings three occasions were to stand out: the annual Wakes Week, church parades and Whit Walks. These provided opportunities for a great many families to dress in their Sunday best and walk around the streets as if in defiance of their impoverished existence and the elements (rain) as the locals dubbed Wakes Week 'the Umbrella Wakes'. Every church seemed to have a brass band, which gave the whole event an air of celebration. Stamford Park was an oasis for family gatherings, fun, games and general relaxation. It truly was the jewel in the borough's crown. The waning influence of Sunday schools, church and chapel gatherings would negatively impact on social activities and life in general as increasing competition from the initial advent of television also resulted in the loss of popularity of the local public house, once commonly acknowledged to be the hub of many communities.

Sandra Goes Paddling

Stamford Park was situated near to our police house and we visited it as often as we could manage. This nearly led to disaster when our front garden gate was inadvertently left insecure. Sandra, who was still preschool age, escaped. On realising that our noisy daughter was unusually quiet, Barbara and I ran to the park just in time to find she had got to the lake, taken off her shoes and was just about to go paddling.

I had completed two years at Stalybridge when late one Friday evening I was allowed to take a phone call from Divisional Headquarters. The Chief Inspector was on the phone and asked if I could be at the force driving school at Crewe for 8 a.m. on Monday. My great escape had begun.

CHAPTER 7

BLUES AND TWOS

Initially Traffic Command was stationed at Hazel Grove, but I was given a separate garage in Stalybridge. I shared a six-cylinder beast with another officer and set about trying to make the roads safer in North-East Cheshire. Ultimately the unit was split up, with living locations determining which officers were to be stationed at Hattersley. My first appraisal with the traffic commander went according to plan until I mentioned that after spending four years walking the beat, serving, liaising and listening to people, getting to know families and experiencing the different shades of communities, I found traffic duties barren of all these contacts. In fact, without this contact it was difficult to see how any measure of trust and belief in this two-way contract could become a reality. His advice was that my current role within the police service was to enhance road safety, apprehend highly mobile criminals and make our roads as safe as possible, which is why I had been provided with a fast car to enable me to carry out these duties.

Losing the Plot

Shortly after this meeting I was to attend Dukinfield Police Station, together with other officers and receive a lecture about the new Panda Policing scheme that the constabulary was to use. If I thought the traffic car to deliver current policing presented an isolation barrier, then this would take this same problem to all the constables who hitherto had been walking the beat. The rot had begun. But no one was listening. It seemed that no one could see what was on the horizon. We were hastening the demise of and engineering the extinction of the hitherto traditional 'bobby on the beat'. We were all complicit and collectively had lost the plot.

Several months later my neighbour, a Home Beat Constable in this new scheme, revealed he hadn't been allowed to walk around his beat as his services were required to provide a Panda Patrol elsewhere in the borough. It seemed that the scheme had great merit, but delivery was being misused. This seriously weakened the constabulary's contact with the community. Trust – an unseen strength – would slowly fray at the edges and ebb away. In the eyes of many officers, the police had begun to lose the fight on the streets.

This scheme also opened the doors to 'plural policing', which I would describe as at least two officers patrolling in the same vehicle when previously one beat officer delivered the service. Contrasted against Inspector Burslem and his Stalybridge style of policing, which at least placed his officers on the streets and housing estates in a deliberate attempt to maintain his collective style of policing, it was a poor substitute. It was a difficult time for the constabulary. It had always relied on community support, but there were many other issues being developed, such as the fracturing of family bonds as social changes encouraged greater homeownership, employment roles for wives and easier travel movements. Without doubt a major casualty was our contact within communities. I am sure this wasn't the original intention of the scheme, but neither was it designed to further the principle of policing by public consent.

A Robbery and Two Ladies in the Night

During the early hours of one autumn morning I received a radio request to assist with investigating a robbery of cash from a taxi driver. On this occasion I was accompanied by a young male police officer who was experiencing this fast-moving style of policing for the first time. The incident had occurred in Hattersley. The caller had revealed he had dropped off two young females and just as they were about to get out of the vehicle one of them had reached into the front of the vehicle, grabbed his wallet containing in excess of £100 and quickly disappeared into the housing estate. The taxi driver had called in at Hyde Police Station to make the report.

We parked near to the reported scene of the incident and walked around the streets where these 'ladies' would be living. Everywhere was in darkness, except that out of about fifty houses where we thought they could have gone to ground one house still had a light on in one of the bedrooms. Closer inspection revealed that washing still hung on the clothes line in the rear garden. They were children's clothes. We stood quietly in the shadows near to this house. Nothing was moving and no sounds were being made. Significantly, no other houses had washing on their garden lines. The washing still hanging on the line told me the occupants were likely to be female and young. So my next actions were what I describe as my Poirot moment.

I walked up to the front door and after a minute or so a young 'lady' unbolted and opened the door. My conversation related to the recent reported incident as I walked into the living room, giving my colleague the opportunity to go upstairs and guard the bathroom. As he got halfway up the stairs when another 'lady' ran into the bathroom, trying to place the taxi takings in the toilet cistern. Game over. It was only at this point that my colleague, a police officer in his first year, started to breathe easy again. Until that moment of discovery he had convinced himself that we would be sacked the following day.

These circumstances explain real live policing. It wasn't intuition. Immediate response was essential. We were lucky as we were only three miles away when we got the call and we had the need to get near to the scene undetected to retain the element of surprise. In this case we free-wheeled the last mile and parked in a neighbouring street. We had searched the external areas of the houses we assumed these 'ladies' would have made their escape to. The clues were evidence of a full wash, most of which was young children's clothing on the washing line, and a light shining behind drawn curtains in an upstairs bedroom. This washing was examined and, except for the evening dew, was reasonably dry. It was the only back garden in that area that still had washing on the line. It meant three things: a major catastrophe had befallen the household to interfere with Monday's practice, the adult occupants hadn't been at home or they had recently returned and they had not yet had the time to bring their washing in. As we stood motionless outside the front window, voices could be heard in an upstairs bedroom. Except for the intermittent howl of a cat the whole area during the early hours of this morning resembled a graveyard.

After a short and hushed discussion the plan was to knock on the front door, and I was to innocently ask the occupants if they had recently heard any unusual noises outside. My colleague was to push past me and run upstairs to the bathroom (which was situated immediately at the top of the stairs) to ensure that evidence, if there was any, was retained. The second 'lady' on hearing my voice quickly ran from the bedroom to the bathroom intent on concealing the cash and condom packets in the toilet cistern. She met my colleague at the bathroom door.

Within ten minutes we were joined by the night detective and his female colleague. As we walked away from the house my colleague's conversation descended into complete gibberish. It was partly due to his realisation and relief that he wouldn't be getting the sack the next morning and disbelief that anyone in the police would ever again believe a word he said.

In 1967 I was the sergeant in this traffic unit, and together with other officers we supported many local community events. At these events we organised and competed as a tug-of-war team with a little success. I think the public enjoyed seeing the local constabulary being pulled around a field on the end of a rope, but at least we were being visible. Similarly we developed teams to take part in local table-tennis and cricket leagues.

One officer had a passion about painting and I would regularly take his radio calls to allow him to visit an artist friend who lived very close to the police station. I declined the offer to accompany him, having no painting ability and even less knowledge of painters. The artist was L. S. Lowry. An opportunity missed.

Eroding Community Support

If community/collective policing was struggling to retain police support I found that I unwittingly placed another nail in its coffin.

The constabulary financed the recruitment and training of sixty school-crossing patrols in this north-east corner of Cheshire. These recruits were generally old enough to have retired, although a minority were young mothers who found that they were well suited to the role and could absorb the hours within their family routines. One of my jobs was to make this change happen.

Six months later they were all in place, and as part of this role I had visited several head teachers to gain their views. Most were delighted because previously the police would often struggle to get an officer to their crossing point and in their absence much reliance was placed on the good nature of parents collecting their children. It was also my first experience of presenting the importance of road safety for these children to a small minority of head teachers. They begrudgingly came to accord with my views after I had impressed upon them that they had a most important role to play in caring for their patrols, which they should share with the police. These posts frequently became vacant, but this shared police–family initiative, which involved much social interaction between teachers, patrols, police, parents and their children, had given the patrols a vital element of partnership, resulting in waiting lists forming at some locations.

In some classrooms pupils had painted their latest offerings, many of which the teacher had placed around the walls. Predominantly their local uniformed police officer had the privilege of being the most popular subject. Staring me in the face was a complete change. What had I done? Every painting depicted the school's recently appointed dedicated school crossing patrol. Overnight the local police constable had become a distant memory. The point seemed more dramatic as it was made through the eyes of innocence; but here was another indicator of social change, the beginnings of which can easily be overlooked.

Some respite was retrieved on Christmas mornings. Several members of school crossing patrols had grandchildren, and some suggested that the highlight of their Christmas morning would be to escort their grandchildren on a conducted tour of the village in one of our traffic patrol cars. At 9 a.m. grandmothers and grandfathers with their charges eagerly waited at open front doors. With polished faces and newly combed hair they sat in total silence in the rear seats of our two patrol cars. Our blue lights and continual chatter on the control-room radio gave the scene an air of realism. Their allotted tour ended some twenty minutes later – much too quickly – and as they ran towards their front doors they erupted in uncontrollable excitement. Not quite Santa Claus, but job done!

What happened to the police officer who previously carried out this role? It was just another example of retreating from the streets, confirming my earlier opinion that we had started to lose the plot. And it had largely taken place without a meaningful understanding of the effects that it would have.

A Lorry Driver Lays Down the Law

As the area covered by our traffic unit included the Woodhead Pass, a great deal of time would be taken dealing with accidents, some of which were extremely serious. The pass was often made more hazardous in blizzards and other severe weather, when there were patchy radio communications. One serious accident involved a large goods vehicle crashing through the roadside boundary wall, leaving it perilously close to the edge of a large reservoir, but miraculously the driver managed to jump clear of his vehicle. The problem with any restriction on the traffic flow on this road meant that large queues formed on either side of the obstruction. The driver was stood at the break in the wall and frantically waved me down.

The tow truck was making all haste to the scene, and if there is always one prat in circumstances like these the next visitor was this person. A well-dressed man approached from his vehicle about 100 yards up the pass. Full of his own importance, he shouted to me to get the traffic moving. A standing audience of about a dozen lorry drivers shifted their feet uneasily. I felt their intensified gaze burning into me, and momentarily they stood embarrassed, motionless and deathly quiet. After a short pause I was just about ready to respond in a polite manner and explain that currently the tow truck was approaching from the opposite direction and any other vehicles on the road would cause another major hazard unless they remained stationary. He was most persistent and becoming obnoxious. I thought wouldn't I love to dangle him head first over the wall and threaten to release him into the water and do everyone a favour! Then out of the half a dozen lorry drivers assembled at the scene stepped the stricken lorry's driver. With arms supporting more muscles than my legs he lunged forward as if he had read my mind. He only said half a dozen words to the man, who obviously hadn't experienced a direct conversation nose to nose with such a huge brute of a man. His face suddenly resembled the cream colour of his full-length overcoat, and without uttering another word he turned and fled back to his car, to hide behind the steering wheel, and we never heard from him again.

Humour can often overcome many boundaries. It always raises its head in the most unexpected circumstances, which usually gives it that sharp edge and makes it all the more memorable.

Fish and Chips and Two Prisoners

Another month and another new recruit was to be given policing experience. I had gone over some basic ground rules and my colleague appeared to be comfortable with his role. The midnight teams of traffic-patrol car crews had stood down and we were the solitary night traffic patrol in North-East Cheshire. I had decided to explain this induction over a bag of fish and chips, which we would eat inside the police car.

Returning to the car, we got our first of the night's shouts over the patrol-car radio: "The intruder alarm has been activated at the social club in Bredbury." (This was the type that was linked to the police station and wasn't accompanied by any audible sound at the scene.)

It was about 1 a.m. and we were on the scene in a couple of minutes. Approaching downhill in silent patrol mode, with no lights, two men were clearly seen walking along the footpath away from the club. I explained the plan of action we would adopt, and as my colleague was older than me and not as athletic he fell into the arrangements without question.

My patrol car mounted the pavement and stopped within inches of the stone wall at the back of the pavement. The first man vaulted over the bonnet and sprinted away. The second man wasn't as lucky as my colleague threw open his passenger door and trapped him against the wall. This left me to chase the other one, which took me around the backstreets of a housing estate. After about five minutes, which seemed much longer, of weaving and bobbing between cars I had managed to get within the road's width of him, but no closer. At one point as I stepped off the kerb I stumbled and fell into the road. Looking up, I saw the criminal had failed to step up on to the kerb on the other side of the road. We both looked at each other at the same time as we lay on the opposite pavements. We were both exhausted and I hoped this would be the point where he would give up. Wrong again. He got to his feet and off we went again. He hurtled through back gardens then back on to the street again. Running under clothes lines in the dark was extremely difficult. I was much taller than the person I was chasing, which demanded that if I was to keep up and not get decapitated I would need to duck, dive, bob and weave and run in a crouching position – not easy. Emerging out of the back gardens and on to the street, I was met with no movement in a street of parked cars and terraced houses. I couldn't see him anywhere. I stood for a few moments, regaining my breath, seeing if there was any clue to the direction he had run in. Everywhere was still and no sounds were made – so where was he? I began to have doubts about ever finding him again. There were no clues. A solitary dog barked in the distance, but was much too far away for my runner to have made it to that location. After all, he had shown signs of being as exhausted as I was. The place was in total darkness – nearby main-road street lights didn't penetrate into this area.

I dropped to one knee and looked under the parked vehicles. There he was, huddled up against the underside and rear wheel of a vehicle. I said nothing and slowly walked towards his hiding place. Stopping alongside this vehicle, I gave him the choice of police action to effect his arrest. At this point another police officer could be heard approaching. He made his choice and accompanied me to my patrol car, then sat quietly and calmly in the rear seat with his partner in crime, whereupon my partner spoke to his prisoner, who promptly gave him a £10 note. They had agreed a bet on the result of my chase. The proceeds of the raid had also been counted out by my colleague and his prisoner whilst they waited – not quite the actions usually depicted on television police programmes, but effective nonetheless.

Prior to this call the two bags of fish and chips had been hurriedly thrown on to the rear seat. As the two prisoners were now locked in the rear of the car, I wondered what had become of the food. My colleague explained that I had taken so long that as the fish and chips were getting cold he and his prisoner had eaten them. As the four of us sat in the patrol car they saw the funny side of their actions. Later in his service my colleague changed his allegiance and joined the Church.

Finally, what did I say to my prisoner as he lay under the car to get him to give himself up? He was given the choice between walking with me to the police car and being interviewed by the night detective at Hyde Police Station, or being interviewed at the scene by a big hairy four-legged animal with huge teeth that thrived on the taste of blood and was totally beyond the control of his handler. He may have been a criminal, but he wasn't stupid.

Doorstep Justice

Another chase on foot resulted in this doorstep-justice case. A prowler had been disturbed behind a house on the Hattersley housing estate. Approaching the house, I could see a moving shadow between two houses. He spotted me and was on his toes, over garden hedges and ducking under those infernal clothes lines. He managed to stay ahead of me for a short distance, but as he was much shorter in stature and heavier than me he quickly succumbed to a firm grasp around the collar as I unceremoniously dragged him to the ground. As I dragged him to the front door of the house from where the complaint had been made, he agreed to confront the complainant and discuss their difficulties. After a couple of minutes both parties were back on speaking terms and returned to the living room. This was another incident, where two lines in my pocketbook sufficed to record the incident, and that is where it stayed, between me and my pocketbook, similar to the runaway-horse incident, in Hazel Grove.

Who was this wayward urchin? He was to later successfully create and direct a construction company in North-East Cheshire. We never had reason to meet again and, as I said, the details remained between me and my pocketbook.

ET Visits

This next revelation about traffic duties is one you may find extremely difficult to understand – and if it is any consolation, I still don't. I was driving at speed to meet with my long-time colleague, who was to continue with supervisory duties in the traffic department. I was driving alone along Mottram Old Road towards Hattersley. The car's radio was silent. I had reached the point where there is a sharp bend in the road. Farm buildings stood close to the edge of the road and stone boundary walls on each side of this road seemed to add to the sensation of speed as the car's draught echoed around the bends. The roads were dry and I was aware of the speed I could maintain safely through the narrow road section, which meant I could maintain the speed I was travelling at. It was about 5.30 a.m. on a summer's morning. The weather was fine. There was a very light covering of cloud and the cows had yet to be called in to the farm for milking. No other traffic was on this road. What could go wrong?

As I emerged from the bend and into another straight section of this road, about fifty yards ahead was an object hovering about ten yards above the pasture on my right. I can only describe it as a flying saucer. My foot instinctively came off the accelerator pedal and my car free-wheeled without appreciably losing speed. My eyes were completely fixed on the object – I can remember my thoughts as if it only happened yesterday. I was driving straight at the hovering craft thinking the next moment was to be my last. My eyes were glued on it. The shock momentarily paralysed me. After only split seconds I decided I couldn't do anything. I expected the occupants of the craft to make their move as I got closer and closer. I allowed my car to continue at the same cruise speed along the main road towards it.

The saucer was about five yards into the field and had started to lift slowly off the ground. After a couple of seconds it gained the height of the tallest high-rise flats in Hattersley. The ascent was a slow process; I couldn't take my eyes off it. What were they looking for? All I could do was to keep watching it and gripping the steering wheel ever tighter to cushion myself against some kind of downdraught or blast from the saucer. It didn't happen.

My eyes were scanning the field beneath the saucer, expecting to see ripples of a blast creating waves in the grass and hoping to gain an appreciation of the saucer's expected direction and force. But I didn't see any. Also the presence of vapour trails or exhaust smoke would have given an indication of when I was to expect to receive a buffeting that might have had disastrous consequences on myself and my patrol car. There weren't any. The craft rose into the air against the background of the Pennine Hills and I recall that the only external lights on show to me were around the circumference of the craft. To give a better appreciation of what I was looking at, but on a much smaller scale, I was looking at two saucers, one on top of the other, with the uppermost turned upside down. The lights were around the rim of the saucer, like illuminated portholes. The actual size of this craft would allow it to fit into one half of a football pitch.

None of this was making sense, and certainly the next stage added to the confusion. As I watched the rising craft it cleared the top of the Pennine Chain, now going easterly in the same generally direction as I was travelling. It was moving away from my position, then suddenly it wasn't there any more. It just vanished from my view. There was nothing that could have obstructed my view. I kept my patrol car moving and I looked around the skies – nothing. It was over. It had gone. It must have been travelling faster than the speed of light, if such a thing is possible, but what was it? I know I was finishing my night duty, but I wasn't fatigued.

There was nothing else for it but to continue on and meet with my morning-shift colleague. My briefing to him about the night's incidents and actions didn't include any reference to the 'ET' incident. In the late sixties to have reported an incident of this sort would probably have triggered interviews with men in white coats, and perhaps limited my days as a serving police officer, so staying tight-lipped was the better part of valour. I haven't had any further sightings . . . so far.

A City Traffic Cop

My first day on duty in the Manchester Traffic Unit began with a strange situation. As I walked through the garages to the parade room I noticed several patrol cars neatly parked and ready for the morning shift. I had previously visited these garages and I knew precisely where I was supposed to be going, so I wasn't hurrying. Suddenly I became aware of the figure of a man standing close to a support pillar of this building. It was an inspector, and he appeared to be hugging one of the internal support pillars. My suspicions were aroused and my first reaction was to ask who could it be and who was being watched? I didn't acknowledge this person and entered the Traffic Unit. I was informed that the officer was checking on the arrival of his subordinate officers in an adjacent Traffic Unit to report any that were late for duty.

My first briefing that morning to my unit was to assure them that hiding behind pillars at parade times wasn't the dynamic we wished to portray in the newly created Greater Manchester Police. My lasting memory of those dozen officers is of their acute sense of humour, their team ethics and their family-orientated interests, which quickly had my support to include organising many annual Christmas parties for all their families in our force social club.

CHAPTER 8

BOOTLE STREET BLUES

First-Day Initiation, Bricks and Riot Shields

This was going to be a different experience, but I couldn't have foreseen just how challenging, exacting, exhilarating and rewarding it was going to be. It was 1976. If my first day was to be any indication, then I missed the point. Was it a team-building exercise cobbled together by some lunatics or a purposefully designed first-day initiation test? A police van crammed with a dozen or more uniformed officers, including myself, was driven to a disused airbase, where one hangar was to be the public-order training ground. Armed with six-foot-long clear-plastic shields, half a dozen officers walked side by side and slowly advanced on half a dozen boiler-suited officers, who at a given moment were to heave house bricks at the advancing line of shields.

Bricks ricocheted off helmets, which signalled a quick readjustment in stance to push helmets and faces behind the shields, which were gripped more tightly to cut off any well-aimed missiles and allow them to be deflected. Some officers sustained cuts, most had bruises and the odd one was unfortunate enough to sustain broken bones, particularly around the ankles. Public disorder was rife throughout the country – usually organised by some disaffected group or trade union that generally reflected support for the miners, or by unruly and disorderly football fans who seemed to take great delight in pitching sorties against their opponents. In doing so, they damaged property including vehicles, and inflicted serious injuries on anyone who got in their way. The streets were often full of decent fans and supporters of different causes who were unable to cope with the momentum of crowd hysteria and violence and were carried along a destructive path, from which many were unable to extricate themselves. United and City home football matches were no exception. Uniformed officers were marched to their positions at appointed times to chaperone fans, who were herded like cattle to their respective grounds. In doing so, we would also minimise the risk of being ambushed.

Parades were held in the bowels of Bootle Street Police Station. The dozen or so officers parading for duty would be sat around a large wooden table which was strewn with official papers and notices. Central to this apparently untidy mess was a large pot of tea and sufficient cups for all the team. The tea was made by an officer who had been preselected to perform this duty. He would make the required delivery fifteen minutes prior to parade time. On the arrival of their supervisor, the general din created by half a dozen conversations at the same time, interspersed by laughter, would immediately cease. Each officer would be given his beat and information about persons or incidents of interest. Some conversation would invariably recap on any previous incidents; the general air of expectation would resemble the television programme *Hill Street Blues*. Each shift was different, but the high state of morale always remained constant. I almost wrecked this during my first week. The night shift was usually notable for the number of arrested persons incarcerated within the cells.

Wrong Prisoner

On one occasion the custody office was buzzing with several males shouting at the custody staff. After listening to the reasons for the arrests, I gave instructions to the custody staff about the nature of the charges to be put to each prisoner. Amongst the disarray and noise made by the initial reception of these prisoners, I was aware the custody officers were showing signs of discomfort. Half an hour later they ambushed me with a request to reconsider the charges. It was nervously explained to me that one of the unruly and worse-for-alcohol-consumption prisoners was the detective inspector currently in charge of the undercover team of officers. Who were these people? The custody team had made a quick change and bundled him away from the custody suite, hoping I would agree with their actions. I did and I continued supervising my shift of officers, retaining that element of trust born out of close relations which fed the shift's high morale even at times when they experienced great levels of stress. I suspected parade-room banter would have influenced their own opinions about the incident, but if their level of camaraderie was any indication it had gone down well.

One Punch

Oxford Street on Friday and Saturday nights was entirely different. At 2 a.m. the clubs would close and 2,000 people would regularly pour out of front entrances and slowly make their way home. It wasn't unknown for some overexcited customers, some of whom had consumed an excessive amount of alcohol, to make a nuisance of themselves. This sometimes spiralled out of control and into spontaneous fights. One Saturday night shift comprised eight female police officers. Fortunately my regular and experienced van-crew officers were on their usual duties. They were positioned along Oxford Street, generally helping the clubbers to make their way home via the taxi ranks or car parks. One officer on her first duty was patrolling with me. We were surrounded by clubbers. It was a sea of young people, singing and dancing their way home, and the majority would be returning next week to continue their dancing or to watch their preferred artiste. The lack of male officers was due to their deployment earlier that day at the Manchester football teams' home fixtures. There was always an element of good-humoured jostling that lacked any malice, which we countenanced as our main aim was to get everyone off the streets.

As it wasn't unusual in this crowded street scene to be inadvertently pushed, I thought nothing of a hand grasping my shoulder. As I looked around I was just in time to see a young male falling backwards and coming to rest as he fell on to the roadway. He was unable to get off his back and was flailing his arms in the air. It was impossible to hear anything he said, but his smiling face told me he wasn't in any pain and he didn't know where he was. Almost in the same moment of seeing this crumpling body

I looked directly at my accompanying officer. She explained that she thought he was about to attack me so, having no alternative, she hit him. This six-foot-plus-tall officer had snuffed out the young male's evening with one blow. This was her first night-duty shift. She was now close to panic. She placed her young black face close to me with an appealing look to get instructions to deal with the forlorn figure now completely helpless in his little world, made drowsy by his earlier excessive consumption of alcohol. She was relieved when I told her to call for the van crew so that she could resolve the situation during the early hours when he had sobered up. She had just carried out her first arrest.

Where Is Everyone?

About a dozen officers were patrolling the streets during the early hours of one winter's morning, which was notable because of the extremely cold weather. The frost was crunching under my shoes as I slipped and slid around the backstreets; and whilst I found very little use for the mandatory walking stick, it became a useful prop to help me stay upright in these conditions.

After an hour of being unable to find any other patrolling officer, I was just on the point of thinking that my radio had become defective when I noticed the police van tucked away in the shadows of a side street. The crew were my regular experienced officers, who not only worked well together but delivered on-the-spot advice to constables at scenes of incidents and arrests. They inspired trust and confidence in their juniors and dovetailed well with their sergeants. Everywhere was in complete darkness. The van was well positioned to remain undetected whilst the occupants could watch the city centre. The driver's window was lowered slightly as I approached. I let them know that I hadn't been able to locate any other officer, and in this weather I was extremely concerned about their welfare. To my surprise they said they knew exactly where everyone was and could vouch for their safety. OK, that is what they were supposed to do, so they noted and timed my visit in their pocketbooks and I turned slowly on the icy surface, intending to return to the station.

Just at that fateful moment a loud snore came from the inside of the van. I could vaguely see the outlines of a dozen officers sat in rows on each side of the van and all asleep.

I continued turning slowly on the frozen surface and caught the eye of the driver, who nodded knowingly and with a parting whisper said, "They are all OK, boss."

Woolworth's Is on Fire

Walking around the city was just that. Once you were aware of the side-street shortcuts you were able to get to any location quicker on foot than using a car. One lunchtime I was required to attend an outbreak of a fire in a clothing shop north of Piccadilly. It was a minor fire, resulting in little or no damage. Another senior officer had attended, and he later made me aware that it was my job to be the first senior officer at the scene. This led to a discussion with my control-room officer, who explained that he had dispatched that particular officer because he knew I had been out in the city since 7 a.m. Using his initiative, he had deployed another officer he knew was available. We agreed that we wouldn't use that officer again; irrespective of any other considerations, he would inform me first of any incidents.

A month later the same situation arose again. I had just taken the lid off my sandwich box when my office door burst open.

"Fire at Woolworth's, boss. Nothing more is known, but we don't think there are any casualties."

I picked up my walking stick and quickly walked across the city to this well-known store in Piccadilly. It was 8 May 1979.

As I walked into Piccadilly at 1 p.m. a scene of total confusion greeted me. Smoke was billowing from the second-floor windows overlooking Piccadilly, and fire officers were training their hosepipes on closed windows. At this point several windows broke, allowing smoke to escape and the water jets to gain access. I couldn't see any staff at these windows, in part because of the thick black smoke engulfing the exterior of the building facing Piccadilly Square. Higher up, on the roof of the building, a group of twenty-plus people were waving clothing above their heads in an attempt to attract the attention of fire officers. They were shouting, but their voices were lost in the noise of traffic and incoming emergency vehicles. It was obvious they were desperate and seeking any help they could get.

Looking at the overall scene as I arrived at the front doors of this store I couldn't dismiss a feeling of deep despair. I feared for the safety of the rooftop staff. The two officers I met at the front door agreed that we had limited time to get them down and to examine the second floor, even though it was still difficult to see through the billowing swirls of black smoke.

Hosepipes were strewn across Piccadilly and neighbouring streets with fire engines positioned opposite Woolworth's. The custody-suite inspector had moved into the control room and had successfully deployed officers from a neighbouring area to prevent traffic from gaining access to the Piccadilly area, which gave my officers scope to clear the whole area of pedestrians. Whilst this was an ongoing situation, the estimated 500 staff and shoppers in the store had been safely corralled by my team and others, and they were being cared for by staff in Debenham's department store nearby. Ambulances were carrying out a shuttle service conveying forty-seven injured people to Ancoats Hospital.

The Café

One of my officers ran to engage the nearest fire officer, who quickly deployed an officer to help with my investigations, but several minutes were lost getting their chief fire officer's permission to enter the building. I needed to get access to the second floor as it was believed that this was the location of the source of the fire. It was also the location of a café and an adjacent storeroom. My van crew and I waited at the foot of a stone staircase which gave direct access to the second floor. We didn't have to wait long to see a fire officer carrying a hosepipe and hurrying towards us. We didn't have any information about the number or extent of casualties, but everyone was hoping there hadn't been any fatalities.

The hosepipe-carrying fire officer was able to stay on my heels as we raced up the stairs. The stairway was thick with smoke, making visibility and breathing difficult, but we had to get on to the second floor before examining any other part of the building. Reaching a large door that was closed and blocking our access, I reached out to grasp the handle, intent on levering it open. I was suddenly and forcibly hit by something that threw me into the wall alongside the stairs. I struggled to regain enough balance to prevent myself from falling down several flights of stairs, but the two officers following me managed to grab my arm, which allowed me to regain my balance. At this point I looked to see what had hit me. The fire officer had seen some danger that we hadn't and shoulder-charged me. Before I could say anything he was strenuously apologising and at the same time trying to explain why he had needed to be so violent. He held me and the other two police officers about five yards away from the door, then trained his hosepipe on the door. He adjusted the water jet to a spray and the water immediately sizzled like butter hitting a hot frying pan. The heat inside the café area had affected this huge metal door and it took several minutes before it cooled enough to allow me to open it. In my haste to get on to the second floor I hadn't seen the possibility of this door presenting any problem to us, but as we ran towards it the fire officer instinctively realised the danger and saved my hands from sustaining horrific injuries.

As the door opened, another wall of heat, smoke and fumes engulfed us, but this quickly dispersed as fresh air raced through broken windows that looked out on to Piccadilly and escaped down the staircase and into the streets below. The scene confronting us was eerie. The café area was silent. No one was seated at any tables, but food remained on several plates at different tables, and we slowly walked towards the storeroom along carpets squelching underfoot with the recent influx of water.

Ten Bodies

A shout suddenly pierced the silence and smoke. One of my officers had found a body, and then another until the count reached ten. I looked at the fire officer for an explanation. He tried to explain that the thick choking black smoke was laced with toxic fumes from the burning mattresses stored at the far end of this floor. This smoke would have crept along the ceiling, slowly filling the café space. The lighting was suspended from the ceiling, so the smoke after creeping along the ceiling had slowly sunk into the space between the ceiling and floor, including the window wall. All the remaining oxygen in that space had been exhausted. During this process all available daylight and electric light was obliterated. This would have happened slowly, so the unsuspecting diners wouldn't have realised the danger until it was too late. This would explain why bodies were in different places. Their positions also gave an indication of their state of mind. Some were not heading for the exit door, which tended to support the view that as the light faded they became more and more disorientated. Also there was nothing to indicate that their deaths had been accompanied by violence. As I examined each person I was struck by their peaceful and seemingly serene appearance in the middle of the smoke, fumes and noise from activities outside of the building in Piccadilly. They all had the appearance of being asleep. Shopping bags were still by the sides of some bodies. I could see my two officers kneeling over bodies and speaking to each of them, feeling around their faces to see if they could find any trace of a pulse, but with a look of total resignation they ultimately looked up at me and through their tears said, "Boss they are all dead."

I turned to the fire officer and asked him why. Why didn't the canteen staff escort them to the exit door? What could have been difficult about explaining the imminent danger to life from the advancing wall of thick black smoke? They had got some diners out, but later it was revealed that those who hadn't had the chance to consume their meals refused to leave, unaware of the unseen death cloud advancing upon them.

He shrugged his shoulders. Tears were welling up in his eyes too, but he couldn't find an answer.

Ambulances conveyed the ten to Ancoats Hospital (two in each vehicle), where they were to be examined by the duty doctor before being taken to the mortuary to await post-mortem examinations. This process shouldn't have presented any problems to us, but it did.

Tempers Fray in the Mortuary

The mortuary attendant was suddenly confronted with ten bodies. He welcomed us begrudgingly and from that moment on was hostile and at best unpleasant to my two constables. Until that point my two officers had been in charge of the bodies. They had handled them with the utmost respect, which was the standard they had set and demanded. They took ownership of the deceased, which the ambulance drivers gladly accepted, and they worked well in their teams. An officer accompanied the deceased in the rear of the ambulance and carefully placed them inside the mortuary. We were not, however, anticipating problems as they set about searching through the personal clothing and property, placing these effects as close as possible to the relevant body. There was an operational reason why the deceased's effects had to be kept separate. At that stage we didn't know the identities of any of them. But my officers had been meticulous about keeping all property close to the body from which it had been recovered. This explanation will give some understanding of their anger in the face of the actions of the mortuary manager. Evidently the manager didn't want to be there; moreover, he didn't want the police in his mortuary. Or was it getting past his evening mealtime? Whatever reason motivated his hostility towards my officers will always remain a mystery. We didn't want to be there, but a job had to be done and doing it professionally would also test the mettle and resolve of my two officers. They hadn't previous experience of any tragedy of this magnitude, but without encouragement they accepted their roles and began the painful job of searching through personal effects. As they were getting on with this job the mortuary manager flew into a rage and began mixing the property piles as he wanted them placing in a different area within the mortuary. My officers spotted this and quickly moved to intercept him. In doing so they shouted instructions to him, but this was his mortuary and he wasn't about to take instructions from any constables. This had become an explosive situation. My officers were tired, hadn't eaten or drunk anything since mid morning and were not about to be goaded or bullied by this manager. I managed to intervene just in time to prevent ten bodies becoming eleven. This wasn't to end there, but for the moment harmony was restored.

Midnight Briefing

My two officers had now retired from duty and we were to meet up again at 7 a.m. the following morning. My radio sparked into life with a message that the commander was in his office waiting for a debrief before I left duty. He had been kept up to date throughout the day and didn't want to cause me any delay. He made me aware that we would discuss our action plans at 7 a.m., but was more concerned that no one had bothered to provide any refreshments to us as we completed our day's work in the mortuary. His anger was obvious and he was visibly concerned, and perhaps it was fortunate that the officers who should have attended to this had all left duty.

The following morning we agreed the investigation team would include the two officers who had assisted throughout the previous day. We would give assistance to a senior fire officer, a close liaison would be established with the city coroner, and the commander would be made aware of progress on a daily basis. During our discussions he emphasised the importance of keeping a close relationship with him and the coroner.

As we parted, his enduring advice which resonated with me throughout my career, was "Don't forget the person with the loneliest job is often the chap in this chair."

Post-Mortems

All ten were examined the following day. The examining doctor discovered that all ten had died through the inhalation of thick black smoke that had invaded the café from the storeroom where bed mattresses had been stored. All had died peacefully and suddenly once they started to inhale the poisonous smoke. Most had walked only a few paces from where I estimated they had been sitting prior to being silently ambushed. The advice given the previous day by the fireman escorting me into the café related to the behaviour of the advancing smoke, its effects on lighting levels and visibility, obliterating all escape routes. All this and the fact no one could hear their cries for help was haunting me as the Doctor explained the last moments of each deceased. I had no idea what could have caused the foam mattresses to ignite, and maybe the finger of blame at that time was correctly pointing at the store owners, but for now as a plod dealing with the aftermath of the tragedy I had my own sights fixed squarely upon the café staff and I continuously wrestled with the 'Why?' question. Why had the café staff abandoned their posts? They had seen the advancing 'black death' danger to their customers and the fading light in their café. If they were unable to convince them of the imminent danger to their well-being and carry out the company's evacuation plan it should have been natural for them to request help from their supervisors.

Whilst I was accompanying the Doctor and compiling notes for the coroner I became aware of tension building again as the mortuary manager continued his hostility towards my two officers. The source of his ill temper was simply that my officers were extremely particular about property from the deceased being labelled, and particularly not disturbed. They also demanded that each deceased person was treated with the greatest respect at all times. The manager couldn't accept this. Everything had to be where he wanted it to be. He reckoned that dead bodies had no feelings. Compromise by him or my officers was out of the question. His continued behaviour wasn't going to wash with my two officers, who were not comfortable in a mortuary in the middle of ten post-mortems, and to prevent them frogmarching him straight into a police cell they both took a break and waited outside in the warm early summer sunshine until the Doctor and I had finished.

We had six positive identifications, which other officers were going to progress with, but the outstanding four would present tremendous challenges. One male appeared to be homeless; another male's sole possession was a betting slip; and we were unable to identify any possessions belonging to an elderly female. The press were extremely helpful and we quickly received information from several sources. However, some people wishing to identify their loved ones were clearly and genuinely mistaken. This is easily explained. Some people wishing to resolve our identity problems were often not next of kin and were themselves elderly. The sight of a dead body was placing them under tremendous anxiety and stress. Visiting a mortuary to carry out an identification added to these complications, but all had a genuine desire to assist. Despite incorrect identifications, which initially gave us a false sense of progress, we were extremely fortunate with all the outstanding identifications. Within twenty-four hours of receiving the first 'positive' identification, another person presented themselves to give a different identity for the same person. This quick and positive response put the brake on any 'blind alley' activity and apart from rocking us back on our heels we realised that we now had a challenge that hitherto we hadn't considered. Outstanding identities were going to be difficult to resolve.

We began by sifting through all property collected that we had attached to the deceased. The betting slip led us to a bookmaker in Piccadilly. The deceased was known to the bookmaker as Little Sir Echo. It was the pseudonym he had used on his betting slips. He was a regular customer, known to staff, who gave vital information about his lifestyle and place of residence. This little piece of dirty screwed-up paper had been spotted by my two stalwarts and preserved for future reference. Both of these officers had an interest in horse racing and knew exactly what they were looking at when they first saw the betting slip, but didn't realise the importance of it until several days later. From there on, the identification of this person was a formality.

The identity of the other young male was proving more difficult to track down. We checked several boarding houses in the city until we arrived at some single men's lodgings on the north side of the city centre. No activity had been noted in this man's room for several days, and our search revealed his identity and his relatives were informed. He had arrived in England from Ireland several weeks prior to the fire.

Another homeless male was identified after reference to his medical records.

Finally, the elderly female after several false starts was ultimately identified by a close relative.

Once I was satisfied with the identities I turned to the outstanding witnesses, from whom written statements were still required.

Leonard Gorodkin, City Coroner

My meetings with Mr Gorodkin revealed that he was a most sensitive and unpretentious man. He made it clear from the outset that he would be relying on me to supply him with a copy of all written statements and to regularly update him with regard to progress. He was equally clear about the order and format of the evidence to be given to him for the forthcoming inquest. This was the beginning of a close relationship with him and his staff, who were also extremely helpful. Neither of us had experience of dealing with an incident of such great magnitude and public interest.

Hundreds of witness statements were scrutinised, with the most relevant providing essential evidence for the inquest. My two officers visited the south of England to secure statements from the mattress manufacturers and the electrical engineer who had recently carried out a maintenance inspection in the storeroom which held the mattresses that had ignited. This and the manufacturer's opinion about the combustibility of the mattresses were crucial details to be examined at the inquest.

I only had one difficulty: the electrical engineer whilst happy to provide a written record of his inspection notes felt decidedly ill at ease about travelling to Manchester and giving evidence to the coroner. My discussions with him were difficult, not because he was a difficult, obdurate man – far from it. He felt he would be totally out of his depth standing in the witness box at an inquest answering questions about his work, knowing full well that the fire could well have been caused by shortcomings in his earlier maintenance work. He was worried that he might be exposed to the wrath of Mr Gorodkin. Our first and lengthy conversation ended in my failure to convince him that he would be treated with the utmost kindness by the coroner, and he refused to attend.

I contacted him again the following day to see if I could improve on my persuasion techniques. I didn't want to threaten him with a summons to attend the inquest, but after I explained that I might be forced to obtain a witness summons to secure his attendance, and assured him that he would be carefully looked after, he finally agreed to attend. My contact with him at this stage was restricted to our phone conversations. Nevertheless I had a picture in my mind of the person I was likely to encounter at the inquest. Like most people he hated the idea of giving evidence, and in the intervening time leading up to the inquest he must have gone through the most horrendous bouts of anxiety, probably causing him many sleepless nights.

The Inquest

Our investigations into this tragedy were completed in six weeks and Mr Gorodkin held his inquest in Manchester Town Hall in September. We had agreed the format and order of witnesses, all of whom had been warned personally to attend, in addition to which I had personally visited several relatives to gain a feeling about their attempts to get on with their lives after the tragedy and to keep Mr Gorodkin aware of their situations.

The Heaton girls were sisters-in-law, and when they arrived in the café they were discussing wedding plans as they ate their lunch. As the front door opened, two small children appeared accompanied by a neighbour. There is never any good news in these circumstances. Their mother had died as the café was plunged into darkness and dense black smoke had robbed her of any available oxygen.

Relatives of all the deceased were suffering some form of shock and hurt, and we went out of our way to welcome them into the town hall. This feeling of sadness and sympathy was the tone Mr Gorodkin struck from the beginning of his inquest. He was extremely skilful, establishing an easy yet necessary level of formality between him and his witnesses. As the witnesses took their seats in the palatial and splendid environment, we experienced the inevitable lull and expectation together with heightening tensions as all the day's witnesses waited for Mr Gorodkin to appear. My officers escorted an elderly lady to a chair near to the coroner, at the front of the courtroom. This was the coroner's mother. During my briefings with the coroner it had become obvious that Mr Gorodkin was a devout family man, and he acknowledged the presence of his mother as he took his seat to commence the day's proceedings. The presence of a close family member sent out a clear message that this was to be an investigation into family issues and reminded me of an earlier and fearful disagreement my officers experienced with the mortuary manager as they tried to maintain an acceptable level of respect befitting a deceased parent, grandparent, aunt or uncle.

The inquest progressed as we had predicted. The final session (day five) was reserved for the electrician's evidence. He was subjected to a very penetrating and careful examination. He was obviously struggling to keep going, but the coroner, without lessening his intensity, allowed him to take breaks and intakes of water. The electrical fault had been unfortunate, but the failure to remove customers by the Woolworth's café staff wasn't an easy fact to come to terms with. Yes, no one could have foreseen the devastating effect of the silent and poisonous 'black death' that had ambushed unsuspecting diners in the café, but evacuating areas of public buildings, such as the café area, is clearly the responsibility of the buildings' tenants. It was clear the coroner, fire officers and police also held the opinion that loss of life might have been prevented.

When I had secured the permission of the fire officer in charge of the scene at the time we burst into the café area no one had any idea that we would face such a tragic loss of life, and such a feeling of limp uselessness as the growing realisation dawned that so many had perished. Our only consolation was a general agreement that their last moments of life passed quickly and painlessly as toxic elements of the black smoke painlessly pushed them into unconsciousness.

A recent fire disaster in a tower block in London – Grenfell Tower – shares some similarities with this tragedy insofar that the effects of smoke and heat can be all-conquering, rendering the would-be rescuers largely impotent. It could be useful and constructive to revisit the drawing board and redesign large and tall buildings to reduce the impact of the ravages of fire, smoke, heat and noxious fumes emitted from some burning materials.

My experience is still as vivid today as it was on that warm summer's day in early May. But I can now walk into large department stores with only a subconscious reminder to check for exits and sprinkler systems. This is a price you have to pay.

Comments by visitors just prior to the fire suggested that about 500 shoppers were in the store during this busy lunchtime, and as it was a city-centre store many office workers would use it for a lunchtime stroll. Included in that number were about 100 people visiting the café on the second floor. Forty-four people were treated for injuries, including six firemen. In total the fire service deployed 150 officers, whilst my officers managed to assemble 100-plus Woolworth's staff in the adjacent Debenhams store in Piccadilly and grapple with pedestrian and road traffic issues which threatened to overwhelm and obstruct the efforts of the fire service. Those twenty-six frantic staff who climbed on to the top of the building waving any item of clothing they could muster, and not knowing if they had been seen by any rescuers, must have feared for their lives, but fire officers eventually managed to bring them all down to safety.

Legislation by way of the Furniture and Furnishings (FIRE) (SAFETY) Reg: 1988 was to provide control over manufacturers and force them to use non-flammable or fire-retardant materials in furniture, cushions, etc.

Mr Gorodkin, 'the chap in the chair', had brought his compassion, understanding and influence to the inquest and successfully inquired into what was a very difficult and trying disaster.

What of my two 'stalwart' officers who assisted me throughout? Later they were to receive commendations for their outstanding work from Mr Gorodkin and the Chief Constable, but they would be the first to agree that all the officers, including fire and ambulance personnel on duty that day, went the extra mile and upheld the finest traditions of their respective services.

CHAPTER 9

UNDERCOVER IN THE CITY

Following the Woolworth's fire tragedy I took charge of the city's undercover team of detectives. It comprised three sergeants and twelve detective constables. This was a new world for me. All the team were housed in one large office. Our remit was to create a presence in the underworld of city life – particularly in the drinking dens of public houses, nightclubs and brothels – and to keep an eye on whatever crawled out of their holes and around the city streets at night. The aim was to create a safer city, with particular emphasis on public houses, alcohol-licensed clubs and restaurants, and any other adult-entertainment locations. Forget the world of striding out across meadows as the sun struggled to make its daily appearance, startling the skylark into leaving its brood on the ground to hover high in the sky and start its reassuring continuous song to its young that no danger was anywhere near to their position, and calling home those ever trusting milking machines on legs, who respond with their slow swinging gait, big enquiring eyes and a low murmuring of content as they push aside morning mists. That vision of tranquillity, now long lost, was replaced by thieves, villains and low life, where trust was in short supply and controlled by an undetectable presence referred to as the 'city mafia'.

Nightclub Raids

Visiting all the city's drinking dens was an essential task to establish contact, and more importantly, to establish an arm's-length association of respect. That was probably a master stroke as it also gave managers their chance to respond positively, which they did (at least to my face); it also gave them the opportunity to identify with their day-to-day disciplinary head to cooperate in bringing about better-regulated premises where personal safety was their number-one priority. Our targets were drugs, offensive weapons, prostitution, etc.

My options to carry out undercover surveillance were, however, severely limited as my bright-red hair made me immediately recognisable. All these clubs were obliged to control the attendance of customers and maintain a register of their presence on their premises. I found that to be a complete myth. Records would show that many club patrons used false identities and entered names such as Mickey Mouse, The Roadrunner and Donald Duck, etc.

A dozen of the busiest clubs were raided, culminating in proprietors appearing in the magistrates' courts. The fine in each case was a nominal amount, but the conviction was an effective stick (if needed) to beat the clubs' proprietors at the following annual licensing sessions. I never did have the need to resurrect any of these convictions. These actions initially brought me into conflict with my three sergeants, who thought these raids were heavy-handed.

Some clubs were better organised than others. One proprietor was favoured by the sergeants as a friendly team meeting place, and during preliminary discussions prior to carrying out the raid they continued to doubt what the likely outcome would be. That raid and all the others went ahead and were successful. Immediately after that raid I returned and had a frank yet friendly discussion with this proprietor. He fully understood and supported our actions, and the use of his premises for late-night team debriefs continued. This principle of impartiality was later to pay handsomely as I believe some of our anonymous information originated from the 'mafia' source – but you make up your own mind.

The 'Key'

One particular nightclub was near to the area where one of Manchester's most infamous scenes of violence had taken place –

the Peterloo Massacre. It wasn't going to be re-enacted – far from it – but one of our officers may have preferred to have disappeared amongst the thronging masses of that event. There were at least eight officers taking up positions in the shadows and deep doorways during this early morning raid. Previous visits had been made to the club, which meant that everyone had some knowledge of the internal layout of the premises. The solid door at the back of the footpath opened inwards and gave access to a flight of stairs which led down into the club. The only light came from a couple of street lights, which in the city hardly allowed a clear view for more than several yards. Two sergeants were in the team and had told me on their radios that everyone was in place and waiting for a customer to leave, thereby opening the door.

Ten minutes went by – no movement. The only movement in this dark, desolate, foreboding part of the city was the occasional pitter-patter of tiny feet as a resident rat moved on to its next feeding place. The officer in possession of the 'key' was getting impatient. This piece of equipment was carried to force entry into buildings and as all the officers on the raid except the current 'key' holder had at one time or another been in charge of the 'key' this was his chance to shine. It didn't happen that way. One of the sergeants gave instruction to use the 'key'. This officer was a popular member of the team and often at the centre of team banter. He strode forward on to the deserted street and aimed the twenty-eight-pound hammer at the lock area of the door.

What we had failed to realise was the door was of solid metal. The key bounced off the door, flying into the road with the officer attached. Both were lying in the road. The sergeant accompanying me and all the others on the raid collapsed in bouts of laughter. The 'key' appeared to be alive. The officer wrestled with it as it bounced across the road.

Regaining his composure, he was directed to have another go. No one could believe it, but the same reaction was played out again. Was this going to be the first time we had failed to gained access into any of this type of premises?

The officer sat in the road cradling his beloved 'key'. He was at least thirty yards away and we could only hear the Sergeant telling him to stop fooling around. He made himself ready to attack the door again, but as he got to the point where he had the 'key' at head height and drawn back over his shoulder to give him maximum thrust the door opened. We were all dumbstruck. I could see a little head appear around the door and talk to the officers.

They made a swift entrance, collected their evidence, interviewed the proprietor and we all departed. That officer was never going to be allowed to forget his experience, but he had broad shoulders. We allowed him to have charge of the 'key' on the next raid.

Fluffy-Kitten Brothel Raid

Several premises throughout the city had been developed as purported massage establishments. Most were extremely busy with clientele from many walks of life. In most cases their popularity lay in the extra services offered. Observations on the premises were usually followed by the granting of a magistrate's warrant, the raid relying on surprise and swift action for our officers to swoop from their street observation points to the front door of the premises.

One particular raid was on premises near one of Manchester's railway stations. The front door, at street level, gave access to underground rooms. Masseuses usually carried sexual aids, which they would dispose of at the first sign of any police presence. Everything relied on timing, communication and response. Earlier briefing of all the team established roles and actions. As the front door opened to allow a punter to leave, two detectives would secure access. The premises would quickly be invaded and all staff on the premises isolated.

On this occasion a young and inexperienced female police officer assisting the team on her first raid was assigned to secure one of the cubicles and its female attendant, but she never got beyond the reception area. She had found a fluffy kitten in the reception area and from there on completely lost the plot. Her caring instincts and the plight of this seemingly helpless kitten became her priority, even to the point that when I arrived in the reception area as the last officer to enter she proudly drew my attention to the bundle of fluff she was cradling in her arms. As I was about to speak to her, or explode, I felt a tug on my arm turning me away from her and towards one of the team's experienced female officers.

She had obviously anticipated my actions, and amongst all the hustle and bustle said, "Leave it, leave it – everything is under control." This officer had acted swiftly, secured the neglected area, retained the required evidence and wanted to leave her colleague with the confidence to take part in future raids and save her any embarrassment.

The debrief after the successful raid probably devoted more time to good-humoured banter regarding the fluffy-kitten debacle and embarrassing the young policewoman than assisting the officer collecting all the required prosecution evidence. But it could have been so different. Having a strong sense of humour, trust and comradeship were essential if this squad was to continue being successful. This was to be severely tested during the next couple of incidents.

'Giant Haystacks'

Any time after 1 a.m. in the city is always a busy time. Nightclub customers begin to make their way home after briefly congregating in the street outside the premises.

I was accompanied on one occasion by a heavily built sergeant as I drove into an area on the north of the city centre. There was nothing unusual taking place, so I parked to observe what was essentially an orderly dispersal of customers. Suddenly and violently my door opened and was effectively ripped from its hinges. In the same movement I was lifted bodily from my driving seat, thrown to the ground and pounced upon by what appeared to be a male. This was prior to the compulsory wearing of seat belts. I hadn't fastened mine just in case I wanted to make a quick exit and chase down a criminal – but after this experience, never again. Everything happened so quickly. One minute I was sat behind the steering wheel of my old car in my old raincoat – hence the nickname Columbo – and the next I was lying on my back in the gutter looking up at something that was completely blocking out the light from the street lights. Instinctively I rolled to one side to avoid my assailant's body presses with his knees. Who was he? What was his problem? At this point what did it matter? He was very heavily built and

I was concentrating my actions to avoid his crushing blows. I was only in the gutter for a matter of seconds. My sergeant, using his immense strength and my assailant's off-balance kneeling position, grabbed his clothing and introduced him to the nearby brick wall. Head first.

A couple of weeks later he appeared in court, accepted the comments and sentencing of the magistrates and left. But he was waiting in the court reception area and made a beeline for me. He couldn't have been more apologetic. He had genuinely thought I was another person. What a relief and vindication for my three sergeants, who had earlier changed our shift rotas to ensure that I was always accompanied by one of them.

Bugged Telephones

There were half a dozen officers in the department during the morning briefing, and I was speaking to the team when the phone on my desk rang. One of our team answered it and held a brief conversation, advising the caller to phone again as I was engaged. He replaced the receiver. Everyone looked expectantly at him and immediately realised that something wasn't right. He was hesitant and obviously couldn't begin to explain what he wanted to say.

When he did so, it was a spluttered "Boss, your phone is bugged."

Silence was a rare commodity in this office, but we had it now. Everyone stopped what they were doing and saying and looked at him or at me. I just stared at him and waited for the explanation. He could hear others on the phone as he was replacing the receiver. Could it have been a crossed line? His look in response was enough to convince us that we were being watched by someone whose identity we were clueless about. During that realisation moment, hearts stopped beating. The belief we all shared in each other that everyone on the squad was decent, honest and kept to the straight and narrow, was suddenly being tested. Was some special force operation taking place which had ensnared our team?

The whole office was turned upside down, but nothing was

found. There was none of the usual humour amongst the team at this point. A sense of crisis brings out other qualities, but most of the team went into a reflective mode and discussed several of their recent cases. We were unable to lift the gloom of doubt that had descended upon us as a result of that earlier realisation. We agreed to act as if nothing was out of place, but our teams 'meets' would be at locations previously agreed in the office and not over the radio.

A couple of days later it happened, although when it did we didn't immediately connect the initial call with this later request. Slowly we realised we were being set up by a national Sunday newspaper's investigative journalist, but we were slow to tumble to it. The caller professed to be in possession of information implicating criminals and criminal activities. A meeting was arranged. This took place outside Strangeways Prison. I was to be alone parked in my car and to wait for his arrival. My sergeant volunteered to conceal himself in the boot of my car. As it was only a small boot, the fact that he did so was something to marvel over. It seemed most unlikely that anyone could conceal themselves in such a small area, so it obviously threw the intended informant off the scent. We conducted trials to make sure the Sergeant could hear every word being spoken in the car and that he wasn't going to be poisoned by any exhaust fumes.

We decided to go with the plan, and after being parked for about ten minutes my passenger door suddenly opened. A huge man slumped into the passenger seat. I didn't have any clue as to his identity. He wasn't about to tell me, but he had information to give to me. We both hedged around several policing issues without really saying anything concrete. He then moved the conversation and demanded cash for his information. He wasn't impressed when I explained the procedures we had to go through, but he listened intently, breaking his silence with a flat refusal to await contact from a senior detective who had a specific remit to govern the recording and processing of this type of information. We had come to a stalemate. Neither of us was going to budge. He got out of my car and parted after he'd promised to contact me again. We had been playing cat and mouse.

My sergeant in the boot smelled a rat. He was convinced we were being set up. We waited, but not for long. Back he came again. This time he revealed he had information about a case he was investigating for a national Sunday newspaper.

Escort Agencies and a National Newspaper

The investigation was discussed in detail with the team. Until that time I hadn't a clue what escort agencies were or how they operated, and no one in the department had any previous experience about them. We had one escort agency in the city. Its services were delivered by about a dozen young ladies, who agreed to accompany and introduce businessmen to the city's nightlife. They were rarely engaged for more than one evening per week and clients provided an evening meal and drinks for the evening, often at one of the city's more established hotels. No money changed hands as the clients paid the company at the time of booking their escort. It was a difficult investigation, if only because we had nothing to investigate and we only had this journalist's word that this was a thriving upmarket brothel. The premises in the city resembled an office, and we found it was only being visited by the company's own staff. We continued to keep the premises under investigation, but nothing was happening.

Several days later the informant came back to us saying he had booked a client for an evening in a couple of days over the following weekend. After the weekend we executed warrants at private dwellings of the proprietors' of this company, including their city business premises, and interviewed half a dozen of their escort staff. We came up empty-handed. My two sergeants interviewed the company's staff, all of whom confirmed their employer's account of their business practices. My sergeants determined that if anything untoward was going on it was likely that some of the staff had entertained some of the clients on a private basis. They believed the proprietors had kept a strict control over all the services they delivered.

The paper's next Sunday edition carried an exposé of the activities of several of the staff. These escorts denied the intimate account of their involvement, and several left the company. Whilst they parted from their employer on a sour note, it was nothing compared to the frustration and anger my two sergeants felt towards this journalist. They had received total support from the proprietors and staff throughout their investigations, and felt helpless to stop the article being printed. I was becoming concerned about their actions should they meet up with him. My next phone call from this journalist was extremely bad-tempered. He refused to believe I had no evidence to pursue a case against anyone and he said he was going to lodge complaints against us with the highest judges in the country. That was the last contact I had with him. I had the phones checked and the network was found to be clean. This had been a classic case of not letting the truth get in the way of a good story.

CHAPTER 10

UNDERCOVER IN GREATER MANCHESTER

Coordinated Raids

Undercover work in the city was usually accepted as a twelve-month post. Eighteen months had elapsed since I first walked through the door of this department. The job compelled me to work closely with the city's commander, whose reputation for being a no-nonsense, straight-talking disciplinarian was well founded. His standing in the shadows of Bootle Street Police Station yard at midnight to 'meet' the team was tremendously effective as it kept the team on their toes. Usually a dozen officers would congregate as the sergeants and I would discuss tactics amongst their active and often boisterous banter. Suddenly the commander would appear and chat for ten minutes, then melt back into the shadows until the next time. Now there wasn't to be a next time as he had arranged for me to visit another commander at headquarters with the objective of taking charge of a force-wide squad of about six officers to target the explosion of pornography aided by the use of video recording machines(VCRs). My office housing this squad was in the bowels of Bootle Street Police Station, but essentially I had loosened my ties with the commander with whom I had worked to bring the Woolworth's fire tragedy to a close. During that time he had shown that all-important belief in my abilities with a level of trust and respect that can be demonstrated by revealing that all those surprise midnight 'meets' had been prearranged.

Driving the easy availability of this material was a well-known national chain of shops. On a regular basis I organised coordinated raids across the force area, which resulted in literally tons of magazines being seized and destroyed. Smaller establishments were churning out videos and many different antics would be used to perpetuate their businesses. It was another world but basically it fell to our team to crush the insects beneath the flagstones. Prior to my leaving the city division, the commander and I had discussed a prominent sex-aids shop which had come to the attention of the police. He felt they were particularly deviant, and his suspicions turned out to be well founded. My city-centre team had previously kept the establishment under surveillance without any success. He was aware of our work, but he was steadfast in his opinion. I have selected this particular case because of the similarities it has with many other cases that my team investigated.

The Phone Call

It was an anonymous call from a male. The well-established sex-aids shop had just been rumbled and it was an unbelievable story. Without this lead we would never have got near to the perpetrators, so the importance of it can't be overestimated. To activate a successful sale of a porn video the customer would visit the shop and be offered specific porn films. One category was available in a nearby shop, another category in a shop about 100 yards away. This sounded like a hoax, but I sent in my team to check it out.

I wasn't able to get close enough without anyone in these shops seeing me simply because I had worked in the city for the past three and a half years and trying to disguise my appearance wasn't even worth the effort, but after a week we had sufficient evidence to support an application for a magistrate's warrant. Things didn't look too good as my old city commander wasn't on duty and I was required to approach his deputy. After my previous encounters with this officer I had long since determined that he would be obstructive in the extreme. The vibes were not good. I couldn't avoid him, but action to pursue the investigations now needed search warrants for three premises and only this officer was available to authorise my applications. It looked as if it was going spectacularly wrong. After a brief résumé of the facts surrounding the warrant applications this deputy picked up his phone and contacted my commander at headquarters. I am sure he must have swallowed hard when he had the story explained to him, particularly as it was given to him in a disbelieving, deriding manner which openly invited the commander to reject the applications. He didn't.

I could hear his responses, which were brief in plain English and left nothing to chance: "If that is what Mr Potts is asking for I suggest you sign the warrant applications." He hadn't taken kindly to anyone criticising his officers – particularly this officer. Had he been in the room and punched him in the face it would have fitted in well with the next scene.

This deputy commander signed the forms, and at the height of his rage scooped all the case papers together and hurled them across the room. Slowly but surely I walked around his office and collected all the file papers.

The Devious Route to Porn

The plot could now be activated. The principle city sex-aids shop was continually monitored. The first customer walking out of the sex-aids shop turned left and, to our amazement, walked into a building society. The next part of the plot was revealed when shortly afterwards a customer turned right out of the shop and towards St Ann's Square. He entered a hairdressing salon, which just happened to hold a stock of hard-porn videos.

Warrants were obtained for all three premises and executed the following day. It was found that each of the purchasing customers had been given a slip of paper as a receipt which when produced would authorise the purchase of the required porn video. The building society had the first visitor, which meant that the second part of the team was in a state of flux. One of the purchasing points had been activated and effectively temporarily closed. As they were effectively neighbours, keeping our actions away from their attention wasn't going to be easy. We literally held our breath and waited disguised as shoppers window browsing, hoping the next customer wouldn't go to the building society but would be given instructions to go to the hairdressing salon. The team in the building society, now behind locked doors, ensured that no one could get into a position to leak the news of the raid to the sex-shop manager.

It transpired that the videos were kept in a locked drawer without the knowledge of the manager and only the clerk had the key. With the full cooperation of the manager, the lockdown of the building society was a relatively painless exercise for my team, except that the ramifications for the clerk had a certain finality. This sort of thing always leaves you with the unanswered question of why do they allow themselves to be used in such a way that their careers are wrecked?

The nail-biting phase was now becoming acute. We were waiting for the next customer, who we hoped would also be given the same instructions – essentially, directions to the second shop. That is how it unfolded. We didn't wait more than ten minutes for the second half of the surveillance team to close in on the third shop. The hairdressing salon was less than 100 yards away, and access to these premises was gained by a flight of stairs, which seemed to take us into the cellar. The porn videos were stored in the locker room and, as with the building society, the culprit was a rogue member of staff. Within half an hour of executing the first warrant we had interviewed and searched all three premises. My office clerk (a woman detective officer) examined and created a synopsis of the evidence. Her expertise was beyond question, but this was later and unsuccessfully challenged. Much of the squad's work followed similar lines of enquiry, which spread throughout Greater Manchester and beyond. The outstanding question was who had made the phone call? I never knew.

Later in this book I describe another episode involving a phone call that confirmed a close-knit organisation in the city with its own law of morality which had no regard for anyone who stepped outside the boundaries.

In that era certain 'hard porn' cases were submitted to the

Public Prosecutions Office. One of my cases was returned, questioning my initial decision. The Chief Constable resubmitted it, insisting that our first evaluation was correct. It was actually the synopsis evidence presented by my office detective, whose expertise I have suggested was exceptional. This was a rare course of action for us to take, but we stuck to our original decision. A written apology arrived stating it was an oversight on their part. You don't get many of those in a police career.

Running Water, Cosmic Rays and a Psycho

I moved into investigating complaints against police officers, mainly from members of the public. In one unusual case I called upon a male who lived alone in a block of flats in Moss Side. His complaint was extremely difficult to decipher and understand. Basically he had complained that an officer had previously visited him and had failed to investigate 'the causes'. The door opened about two inches and a voice asked who I was, etc. Slowly I managed to get access to the kitchen. Here the cold-water tap was running at full bore and all the water was going down the sink. This was to stop 'the listeners' from overhearing our conversation. As if this wasn't enough, all the windows were blacked out. Also he was dressed in sheets of aluminium foil. This was to stop some form of 'death ray' from penetrating his body. Otherwise he was quite lucid. Whatever I said convinced him to withdraw his complaint. We never heard from him again.

Mafia Phone Call and Two Senior Officers Torpedoed

The next unusual incident occurred as I was completing a complaints file. I had just finished discussing the day's action plan with my boss when the phone rang. The ringtone revealed it was a phone call on an external line. As I reached for the phone I could see that the only other officer was completing paperwork at the furthest point at the other end of the office.

My customary response after establishing my identity got to the point where I asked if I could be of any help to the caller.

This part of my welcome faded away as the caller interrupted: "You know who I am, Mr Potts. My name is—. My colleagues have asked me to phone you as you are the only honest policeman we know."

At this point I was struggling to hold the receiver. I had suddenly gone from shuffling paper files to conversing with the city's mafia boss. My colleague at the far end of the office hadn't moved and couldn't hear my conversation. I tried to inform the caller that I was no longer working in the city and perhaps he would like to talk to someone else. That didn't work.

"I want to tell you a story. We know we can rely on you to deal with it."

As I listened I felt as though my heart was stopping. I summoned all my acquired professional resilience, clung on to the receiver and agreed a plan to check out the merits of the information he had just given to me. A divisional commander and his deputy were at the centre of his complaint, which made the information dynamite and capable of backfiring with disastrous results. We agreed not to make contact again and I said that if our investigation squads confirmed the accuracy of his information we should both watch for the local newspaper to reveal their findings; he should expect to hear nothing for perhaps three months. He was happy to leave the ball in our court.

I replaced the receiver, stood up then quickly sat down as my legs appeared to have developed a mind of their own. I knew the information would be accurate, but if any subsequent interventions 'nobbled' the story, preventing the results from reflecting the actions of these officers, at the very least the reputation of the force would be seriously tarnished. By sheer chance my boss was a person who could be relied upon and furthermore trusted to progress this information to the right quarters. As I walked into his office he looked up from a pile of partly completed investigation files, realised that something was going on and immediately wanted a discussion. I gave him all the details – including my written statement, which I had completed after the phone conversation. We developed an action plan that excluded any further involvement on my part, and his strict instructions were not to discuss the complaint with anyone.

Each evening I scrutinised the local newspaper, but it didn't carry the information I was looking for. Days turned into weeks. After about six weeks I started to dread the sound of a phone call from an external source. Unconsciously I started to spend more time out of the office to avoid the possibility of a repeat call from the informant.

Then about eight weeks after the initial call it hit the local press. A licensing-led undercover team had done their job. The culprits were brought to book, the commander was retired and the deputy was chained to a desk.

My boss and I never did discuss this case again.

CHAPTER 11

CENTRAL TICKET OFFICE

In the mid eighties road traffic legislation introduced Penalty Charge Notices (PCNs), or fixed penalties. This was to have an impact on police forces because their officers would be in a position to issue endorsable and non-endorsable PCNs for an extended range of traffic offences. Prior to this traffic wardens issued tickets in town and city centres relating to parking offences. To embrace this scheme completely, new PCNs were needed, and our Central Ticket Office (CTO) was to be the administration centre.

I received the dreaded phone call instructing me to be at the CTO at 8 a.m. the following Monday. I was to sort out and develop this scheme and ensure that uniformed police officers throughout the force received sufficient training to become confident with the new system. The incumbent manager was retiring, but before he finally departed he gave me instructions to enable me not just to find the place but also to locate the precise part of the building it was located in. Although I had previously made numerous visits to the city magistrates' court I still hadn't a clue where the CTO was situated.

Working in a Warehouse

I had parked in the multistorey car park opposite the Manchester City Magistrates' Court building, and carrying several articles of uniform clothing I walked into the CTO using a splendid staircase. I had entered at one end of this office and had a view along the entire length of the office. My first impression was that I had walked into a warehouse. Piles of paper and cardboard boxes were stacked all over the floor. Staff sat at desks positioned in no particular order and the whole place looked chaotic. At this point I could only see female staff, many of whom were dressed casually, which was obviously influenced by the fact that little or no interaction with the public would ever take place.

One of the older ladies broke away from her desk and asked if I needed help. I didn't reply immediately. I was still weighing up the scene confronting me and wondering if I had managed to take a wrong turn. She convinced me that I hadn't and walked off towards the far end of the office, beckoning me to follow her at the same time. To get to the manager's office I would walk past all the existing workstations and see all the staff that were on duty that day.

The only male in this office was the deputy manager, who told me that he was also retiring at the end of the month. The manager enlightened me about existing working practices. He said his staff were not a happy bunch as they were under pressure in an extremely busy office, generally processing PCNs. Letters from motorists challenging the issue of excess-charge tickets (mainly issued in the city) seemed to be his main preoccupation. For this the incumbent manager had developed a numbered-paragraph system to streamline the reply process.

This place was a dump. Most of the staff appeared subdued and unenthusiastic. They didn't want to be there and appeared to have no interest in their work. The windows gave views of demolished-building sites being used as temporary car parks and multistorey car parks associated with the Crown Courts and magistrates' courts. At this point I hadn't seen any legislation from which the new style PCNs would be developed, but the relevant recently published Act of Parliament lay on the manager's desk and its presence seemed to be inviting me to open it.

Hell in the Court Building

So let me get this straight. The manager and his deputy were leaving at the end of the week. Staff couldn't wait to go home. Their work was mind-numbing and the book to redraw their work patterns to accord with recent changes in the law still lay unopened on the manager's desk. As I walked into the main office to speak to the deputy manager I couldn't avoid the feeling that this was what hell must be like. I got some respite when I finally engaged in conversation with the deputy manager. He had an outgoing character and a good sense of humour, and for the staff he must have been an ever present sanity barometer. The deputy manager was the only male working in this office. The age range of the female staff was from school-leavers to mature highly experienced and long-serving staff. Their delight in working as a support service for the Greater Manchester Police, and that a uniformed police office was at the helm, was clear to see. They clearly understood they were not employed to think, and nothing was done without the manager's permission. I had to change this and raise their expectations and the group camaraderie.

Initially it seemed I was going to have a mountain to climb, but that wasn't the case. I found they thrived on encouragement, revelled in an inclusive conversational management approach and almost overnight their dress code improved. The carpet in my office started to show signs of wear as staff released a dormant reservoir of enthusiasm and they gave their utmost support to make the new developing system a viable scheme. Their ability and dedication to complete tasks successfully, evaluate existing practices and effect changes was only part of their outlook. They owned the new scheme and if they had to remain in the office after hours it was accepted because the system was in its infancy. They were aware that the challenges ahead would test their ability to discuss and effect changes into this new system, but it would be a team effort and they accepted their new roles and made the transition to their new working practices a very successful one. My challenge was to design new-format PCNs and introduce them to police, traffic wardens, the magistrates' clerk and his staff. The whole process in the CTO was to be computerised, but the existing staff couldn't wait to escape from their shackles of slavery, and they required little direction from me. With their whole workplace transformed, they were waiting for my new PCNs to establish their computer systems, and pushed on to assist in enlightening and training officers 'on the ground'.

Senior staff created six separate teams with up to six staff in each, and together with the force computer department we identified a computer company to draw up software that would allow our staff to issue my PCNs and our CTO staff to carry out their recording actions. This was an entirely new endeavour. Would the new system work? Would the system for the payment of fines and recording of driving-licence endorsements be accurate and reliable? Could the system be changed quickly and without too much disruption? Then there were other considerations. How would the magistrates' clerk receive this new system? Similarly how would our enforcement officers adapt to this new process? But at this time my most important consideration was my CTO staff. Would they be able to cope? Could we maintain and increase their expertise and morale? The 'we' here relates to senior staff in the CTO and their everyday training roles. Also our practical applications had to be acceptable to our new computerised system. The senior staff worked by example. They were brilliant. Some accompanied me to various parts of the force area to deliver training packages to various personnel and to the computer headquarters in Harrogate to put a face to the already established voices on the phone.

Auntie Modem

On a daily basis I was effecting changes to improve PCN administration. Most of these changes were instigated by staff that extensively used Auntie Modem. This electronic link with the software company in Harrogate was the game-changer, and nothing fazed our own computer-team ladies. We discussed changes to the PCNs and the computer system as they became necessary after we found the system needed to be tweaked, and Auntie Modem did the rest. A couple of hours later the requested improvements were absorbed within the existing system, and these improvements turned out to be essential as issues of PCNs quickly exceeded half a million.

Visiting Mr Philip Dodd, the city's magistrates' clerk, couldn't have been a more pleasant experience. He made it clear that whatever I needed I just had to ask. Our CTO staff had completely reorganised the office layout, Mr Dodd had provided a storeroom in which we could safely store all the PCN computer forms, and we employed a male employee to deliver boxes of forms from the storeroom to operating desks in a 'just-in-time system'. I still had to organise a streamlined system to effectively handle an estimated 300 letters per day from PCN recipients, which hitherto seemed to be the all-consuming task for the previous management team. The numbered paragraph system used to formulate the backbone of our replies was revamped – each section manager answered the initial incoming letter and I responded to the repeat letters.

Walking through the office revealed a changing scene. There were five clearly set-out sections in which staff dealt with the whole range of incoming issues and entered details of all issued PCNs. The managers at each section in addition to assisting their staff would effectively use the letter reply system; the advantage was that the number of problem repeat-letter requests reduced dramatically. But the most telling of all the improvements was the overall appearance of staff. Their dress code had moved on from jeans to smart casual dress, which also reflected their greater commitment and improved levels of morale. They had become a professional outfit.

My next phone call came from the Chief Constable's driver. He was visiting the CTO that morning and, in addition to giving me prior warning, he wanted to secure the best parking spot. Fortunately my previous experience had taught me not to make any special arrangements ahead of any VIP visits, especially where the Chief Constable or any of his assistants were concerned; so when a member of my staff appeared in my office in a flustered state with a confused message that two police officers were in the office and checking through the files, they were told to assist wherever they could.

An hour later Sir James Anderton was stood in my office. His visit was quickly followed by visits from several of his assistants, all of whom were complimentary and appreciated the guided tour given by staff.

A couple of years after first arriving at the CTO I was on my travels again. This was preceded by a phone call on the Thursday telling me to be at the Police Training College on the following Monday. Nothing changes. The twelve-week course started in September 1986 and, as if by some act of God, only became memorable because of a hurricane which during the night in October realigned all the roof tiles on the buildings to new positions across the lawns. This effectively closed the college for a couple of weeks.

CHAPTER 12

POLICING WYTHENSHAWE, 1987–1997

Returning from the police college, I was posted to Longsight Police Station, which was an iconic-looking brick building adjacent to the A6 near the city centre. It was still home to traffic police, crime-squad units and territorial police. It looked sombre and uninviting, and had begun life as a children's home, befitting its current drab appearance.

Initially I supervised South Manchester policing teams, then quickly moved to fill a position in the divisional administration, but within three months I was on the move again.

Police-College Experience

This wasn't before I had time to gain another insight. At an early morning briefing with all the divisional heads the commander asked for my views about the police college. It seemed that no one was prepared for what I was about to say. One of the few highlights of that course was the time we spent with an American senior police officer from the Bronx area. The main thrust of our detailed discussions was regarding actions they had taken to restore order after their recent notorious riots. The interesting part was their efforts to get their officers back into the community and actions taken to restore trust and localism by deploying officers to work in and become part of the many thriving communities. These officers were not to be taken away unless replaced by other officers. I suggested that some of these changes might be adopted here in time, and I suggested we should go as far as taking refreshment breaks in cafés, etc., and not hiding away in our police stations.

Oh dear! What did I say? It was pin-drop time again.

The reply was "Over my dead body."

Communities yearned for reassurance, but it was 1986 and we were still in that era where communities still got what the police determined, and the public would have to live with it.

Both commanding officers at Wythenshawe had decided to retire at the same time. I was summoned to my commander's office and took up my usual position in a chair directly in front of his desk, where I waited for whatever discussion he would embark upon. The main topic was his retirement. I was to take charge of policing in Wythenshawe from Monday, which was in a couple of days.

At the end of the meeting, and just as I was opening the door to leave, I turned to him and asked him for directions to Brownley Road Police Station.

He stared at me and said, "Find it."

One of my last actions at Longsight was to attend a divisional supervisor's lunch at which the city coroner was our guest of honour. About thirty officers were assembled around a large table and we awaited the arrival of our guest. My commander, his deputy and several other senior officers were seated at one end of the table arrangements. The chair next to the commander was vacant.

Suddenly the door opened and in walked Leonard Gorodkin, the city coroner. He immediately recognised me, and instead of going to his reserved seat walked around the room to speak to me. No one moved. No sound was made. No introductions were necessary as Leonard and I stood together, chatted and revisited our experiences regarding the Woolworth's fire tragedy. Others were waiting, so our conversation was kept to a minimum, but this unplanned meeting had set the seal for a most friendly and successful lunch. The only casualty was the commander. I had completely torn up his script.

Local Artist Paints Woolworth's Fire Scene

During this period it was customary for divisional personnel to make a collection to mark the outgoing of their officers. On this occasion the retiring officer's request was to secure an original painting by a local artist whose work he and his wife had come to admire. After some investigations, and more by good luck than skill, I found the artist, Elizabeth Hunt, living in North Manchester. Still pushing my luck, I found that she had several finished paintings, and before the end of that day two of her paintings were carefully placed on the retiring officer's desk, where he, in total admiration, visually caressed the works of art. The painted scenes depicted young children playing football and hula-hoop games in the streets of Collyhurst during the 1930s.

During the time I was delving into this artist's creations, her obvious ability to create street scenes triggered the idea that she might consider recreating the burning Woolworth's fire scene, including the fire officers' actions as seen through the eyes of an onlooker in Piccadilly. Using half a dozen photographs she didn't disappoint, and at a lunch at which she was the guest of honour for Chief Constable Sir David Wilmot she donated the painting to Greater Manchester Police. It was given pride of place and placed on his office wall.

Brownley Road Police Station, Wythenshawe Garden City

Wythenshawe was and still is one of the largest housing estates in Europe. It developed side by side with its neighbour Manchester Airport, and as the airport prospered and expanded Wythenshawe changed from a council housing estate to a population of about 60,000 inhabitants, the majority of whom were to become owners of their homes. The proximity of the airport encouraged the growth of light industry, which is well served by motorways and the tram network. But as I arrived in 1987 it was still suffering from its reputation as 'the crime capital of the north-west', with tentacles of endemic unemployment spreading across several generations in many families. My initial conclusion was that the police, by failing to invest in their communities, had subsequently lost the battle for the streets. Officers either became desk-bound or toured the estate with several officers in each police car. This subtle change had largely been undetected by supervision throughout the force area as there had been a deterioration in our contact with our public.

A simple explanation was that personal contact was becoming (or had become) extinct unless a personal visit was made to the police station. Telephone exchanges had been regionalised sometime before my arrival, which I was to discover was still a source of much disquiet amongst the resident population. The importance of maintaining personal contact and social interactions had slowly lost its relevance.

Conversations between the police and residents had become rarer and confidence in communities had been diminished because of this lack of contact. This had isolated swathes of the population. Younger people, as well as older ones, had become afraid to congregate out of doors after school hours or at weekends, and all groups felt unsafe outside during the hours of darkness. This growing isolation didn't happen overnight. You will recall I mentioned my experiences during the sixties when the police retreated from school crossing duties and, more importantly, the effect it had on schoolchildren. I am reminded of this mistake several times annually when I visit my daughter and her family in a small village on the outskirts of Paris. The pelican crossing in the centre of the village and outside the primary school is religiously supervised at school arrival and leaving times by the village constable, who at the relevant times is extremely busy interacting and creating positive and lifelong relationships with parents and young children. Here at least some success could still be had in complying with mothers' advice decades earlier when they instilled into their children that the policeman was their friend, etc. This fading lack of social interaction wasn't a recordable crime statistic and therefore didn't have any impact on statistics that record police effectiveness. So why bother? The police had much more important things to do than to just gossip; but the serious art of gossiping, which was the forerunner to police owning community tranquillity, had by this stage become a foreign language to many of our younger officers, who see their policing area mainly through the windscreen of their patrol vehicle.

Later in this book I describe two instances to throw the old and new styles into sharp relief.

An exception to this rule was the periodic uniformed foot patrols carried out by an officer who regularly walked the beat in Northenden village, but when he retired he wasn't replaced by another foot-patrol officer. Another officer, usually the newest recruit to the area, carried out the same duties periodically around Wythenshawe town centre.

'Miss Marple'

My first wake-up call was an encounter I had on one of my early full-uniform wanders around the town centre. Crossing the road into the shopping area I noticed an elderly lady who had stopped walking so that my route would have to pass closely by her. She looked like a perfect fit for Agatha Christie's Miss Marple, and as I got closer to her she visually fizzed with delight as she pounced upon me and, with my full attention, bombarded me with several questions. Her eagerness was written all over her face. Her plea for help oozed from her fingertips. She was elderly and frail, but above all she was probably someone's grandmother, mother, sister or aunt and certainly was a Wythenshawe resident. She and her family members might have served and some possibly perished during the Second World War. All she wanted to know was contained in her simple question. It struck at the very heart of our problems, so I promised her that I would take the issues away and try to make some improvements.

She came closer to me, tilted her face upwards to enable her to peer into my eyes and said, "Why is it that the police don't speak to you any more? You ask them a question and they look away. They seem afraid to speak to you any more. It's such a shame."

That very brief conversation identified the demise that we were currently struggling with. Her comment was as a result of many years of a policing strategy delivering a shallow and often sterile service. Our connectivity with residents and families was at an all-time low. We had abandoned our traditional policing methods delivered by the uniformed police officer whose daily travels had embraced the community being served. The effects of this vacuum were largely undetected as the police used their increased transport mobility and technological developments in an effort to subdue increasing crime rates.

I was aware that criminals regularly toured the estate to see who had recently taken delivery of a new television set or DVD player. As empty boxes were abandoned in gardens by proud new owners for the next collection by the council refuse teams they unwittingly identified the next crime scene. As working families vacated their homes for long periods during the daytime they were exposed to incessant ransacking by that resident population whose working day started after a lunchtime bevvy in their local pub and ended selling their illicit gains to others engaged in selling on stolen property. Also the centres of much community contact – the plethora of public houses – were losing popularity, mainly because of the effects of television, but also because they were infiltrated by criminals. These criminals were forming gangs for greater effect, and their confidence had increased in the absence of active policing. Landlords were throwing in the towel and calling it a day as they faced a barrage of abuse, threats of personal violence, damage to their property and an increasingly demoralised resident population, who preferred to remain in the safety of their homes watching television, etc.

Trouble in School

Against this background of gathering storm clouds of civil unrest, I was welcomed to Wythenshawe specifically by two head teachers and a Scoutmaster. They painted additional colour to the current life and times of Wythenshawe residents and their families and the distance existing between them and their police service. These three very different people all shared one thing in common: they earnestly believed in the value of their job and the young people they were educating and teaching to mature into adults that would prove their worth and bring a better quality of life to any area they would ultimately inhabit.

One of my first visits was to see the headmistress of a school. I was unaware of what she wanted to discuss, but she didn't delay in letting me know. Her attitude quickly portrayed a person whose life and soul was committed to the school, staff and pupils, and her belief that after the summer break she wouldn't have a school. Slowly she was reduced to tears. She had experienced several incidents of vandalism at her school and was convinced that in the light of her recent experiences her school would be reduced to rubble. She was pleading for help. She acknowledged that she had nowhere else to turn and I was her last hope. What she didn't know was that as I sat in her office I hadn't a clue about formulating a protection plan, so I left with the promise of returning within a couple of days.

My next interview was at another school, but this headmaster had completely different issues. He had a disciplinary problem amongst his pupils, and his actions to combat these issues were actually causing the problems. He barred errant pupils from entering the school until they had served their exclusion sentence. Listening to his story had taken me into a world I hadn't realised existed. His barred pupils were causing trouble because they wanted to gain access to their school. I sat in his office looking at him in disbelief. I was sure I had missed something. This meeting quickly became acrimonious. I wasn't able to move the conversation from "They are not on my school premises, so they are not my problem." I tried and failed to convince him that his actions were responsible for young males forming gangs during school time and committing crime locally and even as far away as the city centre. Until that encounter the local population had been tremendously supportive. Being a teacher or a pupil in these schools was not the most pleasant experience and, as if mirroring life across Wythenshawe, criminal behaviour in the absence of authoritative figures was a thriving business.

Almost immediately after those two encounters I was visited in my office one evening by a Woodhouse Park Scoutmaster. The meeting lasted for about an hour and he was so emotional that he cried throughout. He shared the same level of dedication for the job he was doing as the two heads of the schools I had visited earlier. His description of vandalism and disruption to his group was such that he feared his Scout hut would be razed to the ground. Against this background he was trying to maintain his group and even recruit additional leaders and young children. He only left when I agreed to visit his hut during their next meeting.

That earlier conversation with 'Miss Marple' was beginning to haunt me.

Another lifeline for residents of Wythenshawe was their bus service. Transport managers had removed their services after 10.30 p.m. because of safety fears and continual damage on their buses, and this publicly sent out messages of authority retreating, fuelling the increase in evening lawlessness.

Scouts Ambushed

My promised visit to one of the town's Scout huts was soon upon me. Tucked away in Woodhouse Park, this Scout building was enclosed within an eight-foot-high chain-link fence topped off with barbed wire. It didn't look inviting, but as I was expected I cautiously opened the door. There were half a dozen adult male Scouts and one female Scout sat around a small group of desks.

About ten minutes into the meeting the sound of loud banging on the roof made any further conversation impossible. Several Scouts had taken refuge under the desks, whilst at the same time their leader, on hearing the noise, had sprung to his feet and dashed outside. I started to follow him, but he firmly told me to stay inside the hut. As I knelt beneath the tables with some of the Scouts, they told me that rocks were being hurled at the roof by local youths who were hell-bent on destroying the existence of their hard-earned facilities. This was a regular occurrence which had also migrated to verbal and physical abuse on younger Scout team members.

No explanation was necessary by the returning Scoutmaster. He was at war. He had devoted his life to enriching the lives of young people. Activities they had become involved in were designed to encourage confidence and social interaction within their daily lives and often by team building through a variety of activities. To allow groups such as these to fold in the face of hostilities by vandals, thugs and ruffians would be simply an act of denial by everyone standing for law, order and discipline at the heart of our British way of life. Something had to change.

Our first attempt to bring about a change in our relationships, and thereby closer contacts with our residents, failed.

Our public phone contact had been removed from police stations to a regional hub in North Manchester. This was a source of daily anguish for many callers who, post-incident, regularly visited Brownley Road Police Station and voiced their opinions about a service that had previously been excellent only to sink to rock-bottom poor. Their complaints related to call-takers who, they reported, were unaware that Wythenshawe was in Manchester and regularly directed calls for help to other parts of the country, leading to inordinate delays in police response. Many of these poor communications were probably the result of misunderstanding by callers who were labouring under the misapprehension that their calls were being taken by someone at their local station.

Establishing a phone number for our local police station seemed to be an easy solution. It wasn't. The service overwhelmed our duty officers, who after a couple of days lined up in my office pleading for the facility to be withdrawn. It was beginning to look as if 'Miss Marple' was correct in saying that the police didn't speak to anyone any more, or was it that the demand for help by local police was still very popular? Probably a bit of both, but there were a couple of issues which came to light. Firstly, a great deal of trust and respect still existed for the local police; and secondly, the public were keen to support them in whatever way they could.

Sergeant David Rowson and a Dedicated Team of Community Police Officers

The custody sergeant involved in these initial discussions was Sergeant David Rowson. He had obviously being placed under a great deal of pressure by his custody staff team, but he had left his frustration in the corridor outside my office and expressed his resolve by saying that others might at this point have given up the ghost but he wasn't about to. During our chat he succeeded in impressing me with his mature, calm temperament and caring attitude towards his staff and public, which would later be instrumental in deciding the selection for supervising our community initiatives. David and I decided to take advantage of our standing with the public and cement our relationships by organising Home Watch Schemes throughout Wythenshawe.

Parish Policing

We accepted that to register any level of success we needed to reduce the gap between the police and the communities they would serve. We saw Home Watch as an umbrella phrase to mean local residents with whom the police would establish a close day-to-day contact. They would be organised in groups of houses or flats with one person electing to be the contact point for their community police officer. This process would allow the groups to vary in size. Some would have only half a dozen members, others two or three dozen members. Wherever it was possible, the main thrust was to establish and develop these schemes through personal face-to-face contact, thereby attempting to negate the original complaint made by 'Miss Marple'. The community police officer in cooperation with the scheme coordinator would personally establish contact with all scheme members, who in the process would have the contact phone numbers of their officers. These officers would daily sift through all their incoming calls and, where relevant, transfer selected items to Sergeant Rowson with a view to updating the remainder of his team and our detective unit for further actions. This presence of a personal police officer who became and felt part of the community gave everyone a sense of ownership in each other as an extended family, in the area concerned and in everything within it, including schools, businesses and local councillors.

There had been years of police-service starvation – a diet of being on your own – so it was no wonder it was rich fertile ground for the changing living styles being hastened. There was now greater reliance on television or video-recorded entertainment, as well as higher unemployment and increasing fracturing of family units, as witnessed by single mothers. A longer life expectancy had swollen the numbers of pensioners living alone, resulting in little social interaction after the working day as these residents retreated behind drawn curtains and locked doors.

Wythenshawe still comprised an overwhelmingly working-class population, but there was ingrained unemployment and the population was overwhelmingly static. The infrastructure supported local groups of shops as satellites to the main town-centre shopping. Going to school was still predominantly a time for walking. Social clubs and pubs, although suffering the effects of competition, were still bastions of social gathering where a healthy level of communication in the social fabric still existed. We thought our wider definition of Home Watch, if deliverable, would require us to set a target of establishing a scheme in every street. As Wythenshawe was reputed to be one of the largest housing estates in Europe we knew this would require a fresh look at policing – to adopt a type of policing our residents wanted. That was the key – deliver what the community wanted and target this vast area parish by parish or ward by ward. In itself that seemed a simple target to achieve, but the police appeared to have lost the art of keeping things simple. Unless we could become members of these large family units and were seen to be reliable we would fail. We also had to be visible on the streets and every other place where our community family members chose to meet. We had to create schemes and contacts sufficiently robust in structure to gain the confidence of the 'Miss Marple' types, who would contact their local police in the face of open criminal hostility.

Many of the criminals were their neighbours. They were a law unto themselves and continually intimidated less-able people. Drug taking was becoming an issue. Policing had retreated and had left many enclaves where only yob rule existed, and the sense of belonging was solely the province of criminals and the unemployed. Many times after returning from an afternoon of patrolling across the estate I felt ashamed that we were unable to meaningfully challenge this state of affairs.

With a semblance of a plan, David invited interested residents to Brownley Road Police Station with a view to establishing a representative committee, terms of reference and a Home Watch Scheme constitution.

Clandestine Meetings

One evening a dozen people squeezed into my office for what was to be their inaugural meeting. The date was St Patrick's Day in 1988. It seems surprising to reveal now, but this meeting was not broadcast and was held in secret. We were in uncharted territory. Amongst the attendees were a councillor, a local solicitor, a local businessman and residents. It was most unusual for a gathering of this nature to take place in a police station and certainly not in the command suite or my office.

The second meeting was held a week later. The solicitor had drafted a constitution, which was agreed, and Mike Satterthwaite, a local resident, was elected chair. Mike had recently being struck down by a muscle-wasting disease and needed the aid of walking sticks, but he never allowed a smile to leave his face. Button Lane Police Station was completely given over to Home Watch as David Rowson appointed and assembled twelve constables (two for each parish) into their new home. They would be the forerunners and trailblazers for present-day Police Community Support Officers. This would be our initiative that would create an impact, involving and supporting our local residents, their families, schools, pubs, clubs, organised groups (such as Scouts) and businesses, including retail management. This same energy and impact would deter criminals and criminal activities and hopefully curtail the recruitment of new criminals. In this way we hoped to gain the upper hand. The initiative would create that sense of belonging that had continually leached away as villages merged into towns.

To get that feeling of belonging we had to devise ways to get people involved by recreating the village effect. We were well aware that families had become financially stretched and more isolated. Street after street of council-owned houses were breeding grounds for criminals and their activities. Many elderly residents and single parents were living alone with a tendency to lock their front doors, stay glued to their television sets and withdraw from society. Gangs roamed unchecked as they set up their own territories (or manors). Previously the police didn't see their residents' plight as any of their concern as they dealt only with tangible reports of crime, but the undercurrent was a burgeoning amount of unreported crime as residents were afraid to call the police and would have freaked out if a uniformed police officer made a personal visit to their homes. We had to break and reverse that trend and give people, including their families and local businesses, the confidence to become involved.

David and I had established a working outline of the lifestyle this criminality had established, and now we were anxious to hit back. Parish Policing was on the march.

The Home Watch Committee worked endlessly to assist our community policing team. They organised an annual meeting of residents in a large community social club with the Chief Constable as their special guest. Most of the twelve community constables attended. David Rowson was the reluctant MC as conversations between neighbours provided a constant background buzz of friendly chat and laughter.

Home Watch Caravan Under Attack

We needed to be visible in the community and we also needed to be heard. The practice of the police going to ground wasn't part of this plan. We needed to be in the face of the community and the criminals. Schoolchildren needed to draw confidence from the presence of their police officers. Our presence was needed in youth clubs and any social gathering that our officers had knowledge of or were assisting with in any of the parishes. We quickly became inundated with calls for assistance. We didn't initially realise the enormity of this impact, but slowly we accepted that we had successfully replaced the void created by removing the constable from school crossing patrol duties with the friendly and welcoming faces of our community constables (PCSOs) whose extended role involved them in all manner of parish-based activities. We wouldn't shy away from anything or anyone.

To get our officers on to the streets and engaged in this high-profile manner I used the only vehicle available in the Greater Manchester Police. It was a crime-prevention caravan. The best thing I can say about this was it had been abandoned by Fred Flintstone and had outlived its usefulness. Nevertheless we took it out on to the streets.

On the first day, after a couple of hours I received a radio message from the officer in charge of the caravan: "We are under attack, boss. Rocks are being hurled at the caravan. There are half a dozen yobs trying to wreck it. I need help quick."

A couple of minutes later, together with several other officers we managed to clear the street. We had been taken by surprise. The criminal fraternity had seen our presence as an invasion of their territory – an affront to their authority. Should we give up at this point before someone was seriously hurt?

David Rowson organised his response. We returned the next day and to the same location. This time we were prepared. Two unsigned multi-crewed police cars were parked in side streets waiting for the next invasion.

They appeared in numbers – at least half a dozen – bristling with confidence, openly sporting wooden staves and carrying rocks. They were intent on teaching anyone a lesson who dared to approach our caravan. As they got nearer to the caravan one of them must have seen the plain-clothes officers in the unsigned cars. They bolted and disappeared like rats down a drain. They would never return.

Home Watch Bus and Michael Wall

Wythenshawe was the headquarters for Wall's buses. At this time several privately operated bus services were still operating across Greater Manchester.

One evening I wandered into his garages and met Michael Wall. I explained my mission to him, which didn't quite go the way I thought it would. He convinced me that I needed a double-decker bus – it needed to make a statement that was clearly visible. If we were to succeed we desperately needed to establish a vehicle that our Home Watch teams could adopt as their mobile base. I was given a conducted tour of his bus garages, then he selected one of his double-decker buses and made it clear that he was prepared to donate one of them.

Two weeks later it emerged from his garage newly painted with 'WYTHENSHAWE HOME WATCH' proudly emblazoned on every surface. This was a defining moment. Several of our community police team quickly became conversant with the handling of this beast and were eager and proud to take it out on the estate. The Home Watch Committee had a mobile home. It became a regular feature in shopping centres, pub forecourts and any residential area where we had received information about any unlawful or unsocial activities. This sometimes included remaining on site until midnight. Requests for visits were outstripping our ability to oblige but David and his team with Home Watch members stuck to their guns. It was the hub of our collective and collaborative community-policing presence; it provided a platform for our foremost objective – our unrelenting desire to engage in face-to-face contact.

Residents, their children and their community officers communicated on first-name terms. They consumed prodigious amounts of biscuits and drank gallons of tea and coffee. The tide was turning. For the first time in the history of Wythenshawe our Home Watch bus was replacing the 1940s style of a delivery van that provided essential and life-sustaining commodities to isolated communities.

Trouble on the Home Watch Bus

Several weeks later we were to experience another disturbing incident, this time on the top deck of the bus. The message was "The Inspector is being assaulted on the Home Watch bus." A couple of minutes later, together with another inspector, we resolved the situation. The adult male had boarded the bus in Woodhouse Park, sat on the top deck and demanded to be taken to Piccadilly in Central Manchester. Explanations that it wasn't a service bus had little effect on him. To him it was a bus. People were sat inside and he demanded to be taken to his destination. The incident only came to a conclusion when our two officers forcibly dragged him off the bus and dumped him on the footpath. After that incident we made it physically impossible for anyone unauthorised to get to the top deck, and we used the upper deck area to house a large power generator. Prior to this we had used a portable generator, but it proved to be an irresistible magnet for local thieves, who would sneak up to the bus, unplug the generator and plunge the bus into darkness. This gave added poignancy to the phrase 'If you don't nail it down . . .', etc.

Those early days were not easy, but the officers David had chosen to market our flagship scheme all had one thing in common: they emulated their sergeant and wouldn't give up. The inclusiveness of the scheme impacted upon the local uniformed officers. They quickly found David's unit was the energy source to progress incoming information. Local residents and others had complete belief and trust in this unit, and with the quantity, quality and content of the information we received we quickly had to recruit six additional trainee detectives to our detective unit. Basically they were needed to further investigate the validity of information and organise and execute search warrants. There would be no hiding place. These dozen community support officers had succeeded in turning the tide. We were now on the offensive, mainly using words as our weapon as we conversed in streets and homes with residents and families, organised social events, and assisted the probation service with their offenders programme and Scouts with their fundraising to help them add vibrancy to their activities.

Our monthly newsletter was devoted to the efforts of this unit and those of the assisting residents. We delivered it to every

Home Watch coordinator. Falling crime rates (after an initial blip) and other major successes featured prominently. We were talking to our residents again.

A *Manchester Evening News* reporter scrutinised incoming police reports of all shades, resulting in us having a wider circulation to proclaim all our efforts and successes. This level of cooperation with the press was previously unheard of, but if we wanted public exposure with a positive police slant on the story it was necessary to allow the press team access.

The Benchill Public House typifies the action we took. This large public house (no longer in existence) was at the centre of community life and social activities. It was in what was reputedly one of the poorest areas in England. One summer evening it was visited by a group of criminals and shots were fired. It opened the following day with our bus on its forecourt. The evidence had become clear. The transformative effect of our proximity and positive social face-to-face contact had become like a vaccine, with our limited resources going a long way. The large grassed garden area at the rear of the pub was given over to children's games and the team remained on site for three weeks. No further incidents were reported.

Street parties were organised during the summer months. They essentially succeeded in getting neighbours and their families to gather in the streets, talking to each other, organising other street activities and essentially reclaiming their streets. I think the ice-cream vans sold more ice cream to police officers and local children than we would ever have imagined, but these actions illustrated the depth of community spirit and tested the dedication of David's team. They also sent out a positive message that criminals were unwelcome. Family bonds and self-belief were expanding.

We widened our horizons, and teams took our positive messages of prevention and community involvement to Manchester Airport. The Hilton Hotel hosted an exhibition and reception over two days. Many local business people attended to familiarise themselves with their local police and the activities of our Home Watch Committee. We were at least punching our weight. Criminals and their gangs were in retreat, and the confidence of residents and the effects of their bustling activities across the parishes of Wythenshawe were palpable.

Councillor Glynn Evans

Meanwhile a force-wide annual crime-prevention event had to be arranged. I met with Glynn and explained the current issues we were expected to promote amongst schoolchildren and residents. We agreed to scrap the traditional non-interactive display presentations and get the schoolchildren to deliver it themselves. The next time we met, Glynn had a script to set the issues to music. Crucial Crew had become a musical. I couldn't make this up. I booked the Forum Centre and it developed from there. The managers of Manchester City and Manchester United were keen to support this initiative and allowed their team members, such as Roy Keane, Ryan Giggs and Ben Thornley, etc., to visit and spend time on the displays. Glynn had involved several dozen young schoolchildren to deliver these messages about serious crimes, vandalism and personal-safety issues and they delivered them in a ground-breaking manner using the medium of song and dance in a musical presentation to capacity audiences.

Resistance drained away in the face of these close working relationships, effectively destroying the 'them and us' attitude as the inclusivity of the initiative embraced whole families. In the process these families enjoyed their new-found confidence by having closer contacts with their neighbours; and by working shoulder to shoulder with their community police, they immeasurably eroded obstacles and boundaries around social gossiping and approachability. All these issues we found present in the many community activities our community police were engaged in, which invariably had the Home Watch bus as their hub.

Initial Effects and Police Hostilities

Establishing closer contacts with the public created several different responses if only because previously the policing diet for 60,000 residents amounted to an infrequent sighting of a beat patrol car that would have been responding to an earlier call for assistance. Initially we improved our communications with the purchase of our own dedicated computer, which solely stored Home Watch coordinator details with an ability to transmit automated prerecorded phone calls with recall facilities.

This was supported by the deployment of two police officers to each parish. Six parishes covered the whole of Wythenshawe and Northenden. Sergeant David Rowson selected these officers and was their officer in charge. Their base was the small police station in Button Lane. They were the sole inhabitants and it wasn't open to the public. David would brief me on a daily basis in my office at whatever time suited him.

My contact with his team was mainly confined to accompanying his officers whilst they were out and about on the estate, either delivering monthly newsletters to Home Watch Scheme coordinators, or at the Home Watch bus, or at social meetings arranged in residents' houses, public houses, schools and many other places where it was convenient to gather up to a dozen residents or specific groups, such as the Scouts, or in local stores, where the Home Watch team would be fundraising to support an initiative to combat crime and reduce the fear of physical attacks.

In the late eighties television as family entertainment was probably at its most popular, which took our residents away from their previously impromptu street meetings/gossips with neighbours and in doing so inadvertently made our job more difficult. In other words families would group around their television sets, stunting conversations within families (similar to the effect of the current proliferation of mobile phones), leaving the streets devoid of the 'salt of the earth' residents, giving a clear run for low-life elements to emerge and create their own kind of mayhem. Our twelve community support officers, whilst knitting together a level of community cohesiveness not witnessed for many years, would rely on information received from their army of residents and deploy their bus in the centre of any perceived hot spots, usually until after pub closing time. As these officers' forays into living rooms, together with support at more organised meetings, began to take effect these impromptu house calls made it easier for residents to report incidents and crimes. This is just what happened. Our statistics showed that initially we were recording greater numbers of incidents and crimes. The main reason for this was simply that our residents lost the 'Why bother?' feeling as they experienced a new-found confidence in their officers. They were eager to help to create a more accurate picture of incidents and to allow their Home Watch Committee to contribute to targeting police support.

Impersonating a Police Officer

Visiting residents in their houses to make them aware of our Parish Policing initiatives was a role I regularly assisted with. One afternoon and in full chief-inspector uniform I found myself calling at one side of the street with an accompanying constable on the opposite side. As one front door opened I was met with a barrage of abuse from the female occupant. All my attempts to engage her in a conversation about local crime and anti-social behaviour issues affecting her locality fell on stony ground. Thirty-plus years of policing amounted to nothing. This lady was not for being conned by anyone calling at her front door. She quickly ordered me to remain on the front doorstep whilst she phoned the police station. She had taken possession of a Home Watch newsletter and stood in her hallway with the door open and made continual threats to me if I moved away from her front door. I could hear that she was in conversation with personnel from my police station.

After a short interval she re-emerged in the open doorway. I braced myself for another onslaught, but as she came closer I could see a smiling face and her arms outstretched in a welcoming gesture. This transformation was remarkable. She couldn't have been more pleasant or helpful. I quickly established that she would be our contact with the occupants of about thirty neighbouring houses and that she would look forward to receiving our monthly newsletter.

Several weeks elapsed before I saw the sergeant who had been on duty at the time of this incident, and I quickly established that he had actually taken the phone call. His explanation of what took place during the phone call was given in his soft Irish accent.

"Well, it was like this, boss. This madwoman was ranting on the phone about a police officer stood at her front door. I knew it would have been you and on the spur of the moment I thought I would turn the incident around so that the joke would be on her. I invented the story that you were quite harmless and that each afternoon you were released from the police station with another officer as a form of therapeutic treatment to aid your recovery after a recent mental breakdown. She was most concerned and promised to do anything that you were asking her to do."

This response was so unexpected that we both now appreciated the funny side of the incident and laughed about it together. I didn't ask what story he had told his officers, but I had no doubt that it was something equally hilarious. It was never mentioned (within earshot of me) again.

Slowly the presence of our community police officers unlocked an otherwise untapped reservoir of fervent desire by residents to take charge of their communities and drive out undesirable and criminal elements. Therefore that vast iceberg of unreported crime together with an existing wilderness of rows and rows of houses in which residents were cocooned and rarely met or gossiped began to break down and melt away.

Our Sunday-morning social engagements in community meetings in public houses with local councillors were exceptionally popular. Bunches of flowers were regularly given to the female community officers (who comprised about half the total number in the team). Most of those attending these meetings drank tea and coffee in between resolving many ongoing issues – usually burglaries, vandalism and late-night noisy neighbours. I often reflected that such scenes would make ale-drinking men spill their beer and cry. Nevertheless these morale-boosting interactions targeting our residents and their families gave us an added bonus: our own officers experienced higher levels of job satisfaction and morale. At this point I should recall that this style of front-line policing flew in the face of our existing reactive policing practices. These were ingrained into officers from day one – not because there was any malice, but because they didn't know anything different and our training schools were still actively perpetuating reactive policing methods. It wasn't surprising that against a background of stubbornly high crime rates a senior officer in one of our divisional command meetings ranted about the police losing the battle on the streets. It was fighting talk and probably done to provoke me into a response, but before I could literally rip his head off I was rescued by our most senior detective officer and I should let his words tell the story. You should realise that when this officer spoke everyone present listened.

He commenced by saying he was going to tell us a story. "You all know my senior clerk in the detective office. She came to me yesterday and wanted to make me aware of the strain our detectives were currently experiencing. She said 'Previously the phone in my office rarely rang, but this Home Watch initiative has changed all that. Now I can't leave my office because the phone never stops.' It is usually information about stolen property and drug dealing. We are inundated and we have more warrants to execute than we can deal with."

During the silence that followed the commander turned and looked at me with a smile on his lips, which meant point made, and he moved the agenda on.

Slowly the crime figures fell away, but you will have realised that this story isn't only about crime figures. It relates more to the people affected by them and actions taken to push back at the loneliness and isolation on our housing estates, restoring confidence and belief once more and across all members of individual households, and in schools and other agencies. The police service had used the excuse of being overwhelmed by requests for their attendance at incidents at the expense of face-to-face contact and quality time with their community officers. This lack of police presence had fed the avalanche in criminal activities. By retreating from the suburbs, the police had inadvertently lost their grip on servicing the demands of the public.

Is this isolation within our suburbs solely a policing issue? Later in this book I revisit this issue again by relating a conversation I had with a nurse during one of my training sessions at Wythenshawe Hospital. Her comments were a really sad reflection on working practices in large organisations.

Park Watch, Fairywell

The Home Watch Schemes included many of the parks established throughout Wythenshawe – in particular, Fairywell. It was a small plot of land that had the former Fairywell Brook on its boundary with Trafford and Newall Green housing estate on the other side. Councillor Burns and I visited it after complaints from residents that floodwater invaded their houses every time there were heavy rain showers; and off-road motorcyclists were plaguing residents with their antics, particularly as the surface in this park was hilly.

Luckily we were assisting a contractor to carry out major works on the M56 motorway bridges in Wythenshawe. He agreed to move his heavy earth-moving plant into the park area and carry out some extensive improvements. The contractor developed a pond to hold the excess fluctuations in rainwater and created an overspill drain to loop back into the brook.

Probation Service

The Probation Service used their teams of youth offenders and slowly we succeeded. The pond was stocked with fish and it was left as a nature reserve. This involvement with the Probation Service and their efforts in supporting the justice system was the first time I had come face-to-face with these problems.

At about 10 a.m. on weekdays the Probation Service transport would deliver about ten young men to the park. Each was serving a community-service sentence, usually of 100 hours or so. For this particular job I was dressed in a police one-piece overall. They were a sorry-looking bunch. Each was in a different state of consciousness as a result of drug or alcohol misuse. They were all given spades to move soil as we were making good the surrounds of the pond, and I wondered just when one of them would erupt into some kind of violence against authority or fall in the water. It didn't happen. Instead they showed what we can often forget – that they are the same as everyone else except that they have stumbled along one of life's uncharted byways. Their involvement in community projects via the Probation Service was an opportunity to climb back on board the route to recovery.

The community in Newall Green responded by regularly delivering bacon butties and tea to the group, though initially these were consumed with great suspicion. I am sure some thought this was a police ploy to extract confessions of crime from them, but the enduring attitude can be summed up by their sense of humour, typified in the remark by one of them, who said, "I see you are undercover again, Mr Potts," as he pointed to the police emblem on my overalls. Good humour and quick wit helped their day along, together with a newly found mutual trust in – of all people – the police. They certainly needed any sustenance they could get as their physical condition restricted their contribution, which didn't quite match the hard work in front of them. But they quickly improvised the use of their spades to stop them collapsing and falling on to the ground.

I found this experience persuaded me to accept the importance of this community support as a worthy addition to delivering justice, as opposed to custodial sentencing. I could also see the effort they had to make – firstly to report for their day's work, then to actually complete a meaningful contribution to enable them to reduce the hours on their sentence cards. The comment of Corporal Jones from *Dad's Army* of "They don't like it up 'em, Mr Mainwaring" seems to be appropriate. Perhaps greater emphasis should be placed on the powerful restorative actions active within general issues embraced by the positive transformative effects of proximity, developing mutual trust within the community and, maybe most importantly, actively demonstrating that humans need to know they belong.

Man Down

Not everyone supported the reclamation of this wilderness. On one occasion as I was preparing an area for grass seeding I heard a thud as something hit the ground a few feet away. The next thud was nearer. I realised that someone was shooting a firearm and I concluded that it was coming from the flats on the border of the park. I lay on the ground and waited. I was either going to be hit or my actions feigning injury would succeed. It worked. After five minutes I retreated to a safer distance.

Within twenty minutes David Rowson and his team had spoken to sufficient residents to scare off this misguided resident. We never had any repeat incidents. Throughout I was assisted by many stalwarts amongst local residents and particularly David Hilton, a resident of Woodhouse Park.

Flooding became a thing of the past and on one of my last days before concluding my work in the park, during the height of summer, I was to witness a swift swooping between the trees around the edge of the pond, diving as if on a collision course with the pond, scooping up water in its beak then rising from the surface to soar high into the sky once more. The whole movement took seconds, then this black majestic master of the skies returned to its lofty position to resume its bobbing, weaving, ducking and diving above Fairywell. A search of the skies showed that a colony of swifts had successfully made this their habitat. That sight alone repaid the efforts of all those who had contributed to the construction of this park.

A Ten-Year-Old Boy in the Cells

The son of our Fairywell Park project manager had been proving troublesome within his family circle and his father appealed to us for help. We devised a plan whereby we would contrive the arrest of our park project manager and his son. As the cells at Brownley Road Police Station were no longer in use, we placed the young boy in the cells, then slammed and locked the door. The father remained sitting outside the cell, in the corridor. Fifteen minutes went by, then the father and I decided that was long enough to make the lesson effective. The boy was relieved to get released, and as he left the station he was gripping his father's hand as if stuck like glue. He never again disobeyed his parents, and his father believed the experience had been life-changing in a positive way.

Whilst this was an unusual request, it demonstrated the extended family influence and support of the police working in close contact within their communities.

A Casual Visitor

One evening as I was about to leave duty for the day the officer on the front desk in the police station phoned me to say he had directed a man to my office and he was on his way. The shuffling of feet came ever closer and a face appeared from behind the door. He instantly introduced himself, but he needn't have done as I knew exactly who he was. Wythenshawe's Member of Parliament, Alf Morris, was now sitting in my office, chatting away as if we were old mates. His objective was to glean more information about our community policing initiatives and voice his support for our work in the community.

He visited several times, always around the same time, never with any pomp or ceremony. As his generous body rested comfortably in my office chair I listened to his well-informed conversation and quickly gave him an update on our policing issues – even the ones we were struggling to bring to a successful conclusion. It was easy to see why most residents in Wythenshawe were his staunch supporters and why he was such a popular MP. Later he was to become Lord Morris.

The Home Secretary Visits

My immediate boss and I were informed that Michael Howard, MP, at that time the Home Secretary, was to spend the day with us. The difficulty was that throughout my service I had visited many prisoners in their cells. Many of these were reoffenders. In other words, being arrested and given custodial sentences had not impressed them and they were unlikely to change their ways. Also over the years I had checked scores of custody sheets and couldn't help noticing that eight out ten offenders arrested in Wythenshawe had a previous criminal record. The system wasn't working. These experiences had coloured my views about the prison system and had left me feeling that many of these offenders had been neglected by an ineffectual system. In some cases prison seemed to harden their opinions against trying to regain their initial law-abiding existence.

In fact I was unable to see the merits of short-term custodial sentences in cases where community sentences required greater effort by the offender with usually more positive outcomes.

Unfortunately the reputation of Michael Howard, MP, didn't seem to be of that view, so we kept our conversations to the subjects of community cohesion and the role of our community police officers on one of the country's largest housing estates. We impressed on the Home Secretary that the role of these officers didn't require police powers. In fact, to have them would only draw them away from their major role of delivering community policing by closer contact with our 'Miss Marple' types, sowing confidence and extending the 'family' image whilst they gave essential advice, collected information to nip criminal acts in the bud and stamped their authority amongst criminal elements. This was our transformative effect. My only concession was to allow our community policing team to assist our detectives about two days per month, when extra numbers were needed, to act on information received and carry out dawn raids. Then they would essentially become property handlers and were highly visible in the streets as part of a law-enforcing team.

The Home Secretary had wanted to see how effective our methods were and, as a good listener, he impressed us as a highly approachable Home Secretary. He would later create the Police Community Support Officers Scheme, essentially to liaise with residents and their families and largely replicate our scheme. We explained all of our activities and the supportive roles of our residents, their families and the Home Watch Committee. His response was most encouraging. He immediately recognised the importance of this consultative, consuming and transformative effect of proximity as we strove to deliver Parish Policing 'on your street'.

Michael Howard, MP, later became Lord Howard.

'Inspector Jigsaw'

One of our inspectors had been posted to us from motorway duties on a temporary basis. Brownley Road Police Station was characterised by narrow corridors and a narrow stairway to the upper floor. One day as I was climbing the stairs an inspector and I were walking in opposite directions. We exchanged our normal welcoming chat, then as I drew level with him his face seemed to disintegrate and I saw jigsaw-like lines across the whole of his face. We had finished our greeting and passed shoulder to shoulder. Both of us continued walking in opposite directions.

I was speechless, totally alarmed and unnerved, but continued walking to my office door. David Barlow, my boss, was sitting at his desk so I walked into his office and sat near his desk. He immediately recognised that something had unsettled me and came to my aid. I related my story to him, daft as it may have seemed, but he took it extremely seriously. Neither of us had a clue what was going on. Explanations for what had happened or what it could have meant remained up in the air. We couldn't shed any light on any of it. David made a cup of tea as he could see that visibly I was still shaken, then we agreed not to dwell on this incident, forget it had actually happened and move on.

Driving into work one morning a couple of months later, I heard my car radio announce that there had been a fatal shooting of a police inspector at a service station on the M62 in Greater Manchester. Shortly after my unaccountable incident, this inspector had been transferred back to motorway duties – but it couldn't have been him, I kept telling myself. Surely they had made a mistake; surely they had got the identity wrong! These were the thoughts racing around my brain as I approached my office.

David Barlow was stood waiting for me. As our eyes met I knew it hadn't been a mistake – it was our former colleague. He knew this could be a difficult experience for me to absorb and repeatedly assured me that we couldn't have done anything differently to change the outcome. I knew his advice was correct; nevertheless, even for the most seasoned and hardened police officers this was a difficult situation to grapple with. We both did and moved on, but periodically I momentarily relive the experience. The recurring question about whether or not any different actions at the time would have changed matters always ends up with no and convinces me that we couldn't have prevented the tragedy, which involved a first-rate police officer and the most congenial family man you could ever wish to meet.

Salford University

I could never have imagined myself attending a degree course at any university, but I had been persuaded by another officer to give it a try. My motivation was simply to equip myself with an ability to deliver our community policing initiative. Were we doing it in the best way or was there something we were seriously overlooking? I signed up for a course in marketing in the late 1980s as the promotional correspondence appeared to target the needs of customers, which at that time was an alien concept in the police service. I needed to take this marketing message to our community police officers and to all those living, working and in business in Wythenshawe.

Initially I thought I had enrolled for a foreign-language course, but gradually things became clearer. It was like that transitional state at dawn when sunlight illuminates the horizon, often triggering re-energised activities in the daily fight for survival in the animal (or human) world – but slowly understanding washed over me and my enlightenment increased to match the bolder light of the day. This was entirely due to the patience and skill of the university's lecturers and two course colleagues who persistently walked me up and down the aisles of the library as I searched for that elusive book.

In the early nineties I graduated with a Master of Science degree in marketing, and with it the lessons had been learnt to drive our initiatives forward.

CHAPTER 13

VISITING THE PALACE

There was nothing unusual about my working day until I received a phone call from my wife, Barbara, trying to pass a message to me. She was totally incoherent. After several attempts to rerun the message, and not getting to any clearer interpretation of what she was trying to say, I ended the phone call by saying I would be home in thirty minutes.

As I drove home after countless times of rerunning the message in my mind, the best conclusion I could arrive at was that I had received a letter which gave details of a summons to attend at Buckingham Palace. There was nothing else to do but to study the contents of the letter myself.

As I opened the front door Barbara was stood shaking from head to toe and she was still unable to make sense of the letter.

It was a summons to attend at Buckingham Palace, where Her Majesty the Queen was to present me with a medal for outstanding service to the communities of Wythenhawe. Barbara and I read the letter several times. It must be a mistake, I thought – someone had designed some elaborate hoax.

I wasn't going to be taken in by it and I decided to phone the Buckingham Palace number which appeared at the head of the letter. My phone call was answered immediately and by a most courteous male who had no difficulty in recognising my plight as I explained that I thought his office had made a mistake. He only asked me to confirm my name and date of birth.

Then his response was immediate: "No mistake, sir. You have been awarded the Queen's Police Medal for outstanding services to the communities of Wythenshawe. Details of the award ceremony will be sent through the post at a later date. Meanwhile, until details appear in *The Times* newspaper on New Year's Day you are asked to refrain from passing this information on to anyone else."

I couldn't keep Barbara in suspense any longer and immediately I replaced the receiver I tried to convince her that this was a genuine summons to the palace. But how did this happen? I would have to wait for the public announcement on New Year's Day 1997, which was still three weeks away. Keeping this information to ourselves left us both confused, except that we knew we were not to disclose this information to anyone. I found myself counting the days and wondering if I would have to speak to the press and other officers.

Eventually we got there. Everyone I had been working with was most supportive. It was equally in recognition of their services, just as much as mine and Barbara's, and after discussions with the Home Watch team and others I marked the occasion with a reception at Wythenshawe Hall. Most of the team, including police and the Home Watch Committee, managed to attend. We had all worked together for the past decade and the effects of our Parish Policing initiative had been driven home on the front line by Sergeant David Rowson. His enduring ability to make sense of our discussions was to his lasting credit. In recognition of their efforts Barbara and I also had lunch with the Chief Constable, Sir David Wilmot, and his wife, Ann, at police headquarters. What we thought would be a daunting experience was anything but. The afternoon flew past in a flash against a background of good-humoured non-stop conversation. Most of the celebrations at this time overwhelmed Barbara, but we both fondly remember this occasion and the kindness of Sir David and Ann.

Buckingham Palace

Our date to visit the palace was during early summer that year, 1997. We had arranged to meet our daughter Sandra, who was resident in France, in London. Everything went like clockwork. Prior to attending this ceremony I had received a phone call from an officer who had previously attended a similar occasion at the palace. He stressed upon me that the best advice he had received was to arrive at the palace prior to the time on the invitation. We did just that – we had nearly an hour to spare. The taxi driver dropped us at the front gates, where we were met by a uniformed attendant who directed us to walk towards the front door. This was a slow walk as we tried to soak up the occasion and atmosphere. No other people had arrived when we got there, but standing on the steps of the palace and looking back to the entrance gates I could see other guests had started to arrive. Walking inside the entrance area, our eyes were immediately drawn to the splendid paintings hanging on the walls. They depict rural scenes and people (adults, children and animals) of previous centuries and are no doubt by famous artists. Barbara and Sandra were escorted to an assembly room comprising many rows of seating, and they took up their positions in the second row. Their view of proceedings was excellent and, though I wasn't to know it at that time, they were in full view of the recording cameras, giving them a prominent position on the video recording of the occasion. The recording clearly shows Barbara and Sandra watching the whole ceremony.

Meanwhile the award recipients were ushered into a holding area which had walls equally adorned with huge tapestry-type paintings. I found myself standing shoulder to shoulder with celebrities such as the entertainer and singer Frankie Vaughan and the actor Michael York. We were quietly strolling around this huge reception area and trying to soak up the atmosphere.

Another police officer was also waiting in this area. My conversations with him were not what I expected. He had arrived at his hotel the previous evening and decided to unpack his uniform. He was horrified to find that he had failed to pack his uniform trousers. Total panic set in. He resolved his predicament by getting a colleague to visit his home late at night before the day of the ceremony and drive towards London from somewhere in East Anglia. Meanwhile he drove from London to meet his colleague halfway. The only casualty was that he hadn't managed to get much sleep, but 'All's well that ends well.'

HRH Prince Charles and the Spice Girls

I waited in a side room with several men and women, and on the command to enter the presentation area I walked into the assembly hall. For the first time I saw HRH Prince Charles stood at the end of the room under the gaze of several hundred seated guests. On the balcony above the guests and facing HRH Prince Charles an orchestra was softly playing chamber music. The atmosphere was electric, but it was obvious that staff organising these functions had become most professional. Everything went according to their plan.

I strode forward, shook hands with HRH Prince Charles and had a short conversation with him. I was struck by his sincerity and observed that he was able to stay on the same script and impress everyone in the same manner at this ceremony.

He congratulated me, stressed the importance of staying engaged and involved in community projects and concluded our chat by saying, "I am coming to Manchester this afternoon and I am going to meet the Spice Girls. Isn't that exciting?"

Our trip to London ended all too soon. We had all enjoyed the occasion and felt deeply privileged and honoured to have been chosen to represent the officers delivering our community policing efforts and all the residents and families in Wythenshawe.

Several months later I retired from the police service after thirty-five years, and to mark the occasion the Home Watch chair organised a gathering of our community police and supporters in the old yet still magnificent Wythenshawe Hall. During my thirty-five years' service as a police officer I worked with many first-rate officers and support staff. They stand out like the first blooms of spring after a particularly bitter winter. I was drawn to them and was privileged to share in their outgoing, caring, positive and professional mannerisms. David Barlow was in this company – a giant amongst his contemporaries.

CHAPTER 14

THE NHS, CRIME MANAGEMENT AND A CYCLING CLUB

Throughout my final ten years' police service at Wythenshawe I had been plagued by the proliferation of crime, particularly the attacks on cars at Wythenshawe Hospital. I had attended for several years as their police representative and had developed an understanding of the opportunities for criminals to attack staff cars and the hospital; so when I took charge of security I knew what actions were needed and, perhaps more importantly, I was acquainted with some relevant personnel.

During my first meeting with the hospital trust's general manager he took great pains to explain the existence of the hierarchy currently controlling the NHS. It was 1997. I think my look of disbelief was sufficient for him to repeat his explanation. I just couldn't believe the hurdles that obstructed progress. I felt that I had taken a step back in time. Fortunately I had previously developed the Hospital Watch Committee, which had given me a platform to regularly meet with hospital managers. In fact, the first fundraising effort we carried out provided funding for the CCTV and electronic door security system to protect the maternity units. Much of the bucket rattling around Wythenshawe was carried out by Scout groups. The Hospital Watch Committee and hospital management shared the total cost of £10,000. These actions raised the profile of security officers amongst other staff as they were seen to be more professional, informed, involved and responsive, and this also had the welcome effect of improving their own morale, feeling of belonging and motivation.

Although the hospital management at that time employed a

team of 24/7 security officers, nothing they could do impacted against the frequency of car crime, vandalism and violent assaults, particularly in the hospital's accident and emergency department (A & E).

One of my earliest introductions to working life outside the police service was a visit to the security office with the general manager. We walked into the security office, where one nine-inch CCTV screen was working and three others were blank. An ensuing conversation with the senior security officer took place in the public area of the outpatients department. It was so heated I was on the verge of summoning the police to arrest both of them. Changes were needed to professionalise their equipment and working practices, and to this end the general manager always gave me his full support.

Actions Taken

Hospital Watch volunteers, who were local residents, assisted in the hospital's security control room, and their presence was highlighted by a large sign outside their office advertising their presence and their association with the Greater Manchester Police. Many of these were the same people that had been actively engaged for many hours raising funds to improve maternity security. To improve their ability to communicate I had obtained a dozen personal radio sets for both control rooms at Wythenshawe and Withington Hospitals. The volunteers quickly familiarised themselves with the hospital buildings, and the improvement in communications moved the whole security-service efficiency to much higher levels. Local police and PCSOs regularly visited and would ultimately spend time and gain much needed intelligence from both hospitals' CCTV surveillance cameras. This team's work ethic was a mirror image of that existing in the communities of Wythenshawe.

Initially the main visitors' car park at Wythenshawe was flanked by rapidly becoming obsolete and disused wooden hospital buildings, which gave criminals excellent cover. Like vultures they would circle and swoop on vehicles – particularly those with items of interest left on view inside them. It appeared that a common practice, particularly during the weekend evenings, was for patients injured as a result of violent incidents to be closely followed to A & E by an entourage of like-minded colleagues who were still carrying their weapons – usually knives. As our security officers were in evidence in these reception areas they abandoned their knives amongst the shrubbery around the car parks. A collection of these were kept within a display case to remind staff at their training sessions of their need to remain vigilant. Otherwise the shale-surfaced car park was strewn with broken glass to evidence previous successful criminal attacks. No evidence was ever gathered to arrest any perpetrators and none were ever intercepted or caught in the act of committing crime.

Similarly incidents of theft from within the hospital were rife, also against a background of inconclusive investigations.

A couple of contractors currently engaged on building work at the hospital offered to donate their portable perimeter wire fencing, which had effectively protected their site materials. This had to be repositioned along hospital boundaries if we were to succeed in stemming the tide of marauding criminals. It was done by as many volunteers as I could find. This included several security officers who stayed on duty beyond their twelve-hour shifts. It was successful and remains in place some twenty years later.

I quickly presented a scheme to the government to install a system of CCTV cameras and recording systems. In total both hospitals were given a grant of £250,000. This comprehensive system transformed the level of safety, security and staff confidence, particularly for those leaving their shifts late in the evening and in poor visibility in and around Wythenshawe and Withington Hospitals.

Police Horses Deployed

To improve our visibility and response, the trust provided a large wooden shed for the use of two police horses as the distance to the hospital from the police stables did not make it feasible to complete a round journey in one day. The horses proved to be very effective and their presence probably frightened most of the local criminals away. One of the mounted officers' most popular objectives was their presence in the car park outside the children's wards. It often seemed to me that it was difficult to decide whether these two huge horses standing motionless and peering through the windows into the eyes of the children were enjoying the experience more than the children, but their departure was always another scene of great excitement.

Electrifying Staff-Car-Park Fences

During this time Wythenshawe Hospital was developing a large-capacity staff car park on its borders. Against a background of unchecked criminality there was a great deal of well-founded concern by staff about the safety of their vehicles. To ameliorate their concerns I proposed radical measures to spread our CCTV coverage to this car park and enclose it within a ten-foot electric chain-link fence. The reception of this proposal was one of eyes popping out of sockets and mouths gaping open in disbelief. It was successfully installed, and from its inception the car park was known locally as Jurassic. Staff put the car park to good use and quickly forgot the electric-fence issue.

I decided to rely on my previous experience of working with electric fences and the effect they have on animals. Almost instantly animals recognise the electric fence, give it their utmost respect and will graze within an inch without touching it. I always felt that their secret in remaining free from electric shocks is that they can hear the electric current flowing through the wire fencing. If the battery suddenly expires their level of respect remains the same. In other words, testing the fence by touching it is not an option.

The hospital contractor and I decided the effect of this fence would not be diminished if it remained switched off, but this would not be disclosed to anyone. A couple of months went by – no criminal attacks had been recorded – then I received two complaints from members of staff. They had touched the fence and received burns to their hands. They received treatment in A & E and were later discharged. They were reminded that the signage was adequate and any neglect was theirs. There was no logic in anyone going out of their way to test the effectiveness of this fence. The contractor and I quickly tested the fence just in case something had malfunctioned, but it hadn't. It still stood in all its glory and never again carried the electric current. We had experienced our first taste of the 'Luddite' element within this large organisation, which probably reflects similar attitudes elsewhere. The fence remained switched off and the allegedly injured staff were told to formalise a complaint. None was forthcoming.

Another first also came at this location and completely out of the blue. Whilst working on this project the security supervisor, after listening intently to my description of the many different trees growing in this 1,500-space car park, suddenly and with a little embarrassment asked if I could explain to him how he should recognise which of the trees were actually oak. At first I thought he was pulling my leg, but it was obvious that he was being serious. He was perhaps typical of those with a city upbringing. He would later become the trust's car-park manager for about ten years, during which he volunteered to spend many hours fundraising for trust initiatives. He worked tirelessly erecting a perimeter fence which effectively kept out our undesirable criminal invaders, and he completed remedial groundwork which effectively established a network of drains designed to capture surface rainwater.

Hospital Special Constables

Two members of staff volunteered their time and were fully trained by the Greater Manchester Police. They contributed a huge number of hours patrolling the hospital and were rewarded by witnessing a boost in the confidence of existing security officers and PCSOs and a return to a level of tranquillity expected in hospitals. This allowed their role in the face of fewer incidents of violence to be extended to other duties across Wythenshawe, but still underpinning the strategy of maintaining the issues that presented the hospital as family-friendly and safe.

Responding to Incidents

With camera surveillance inside and outside hospital buildings, the subject of our security response became an issue. The sites at Withington and Wythenshawe had two large battery-powered buggies currently in use. These buggies were more at home on hospital corridors, but totally inadequate in an open environment as their top speed was slightly in excess of that of an off-colour hedgehog. (I did say I felt I had stepped back in time.) Two small vans were provided for external use, so response to incidents could now be measured in several minutes. Criminals started to get the message. Security officers were on a roll and criminal attacks on visitors' cars were becoming a thing of the past. These small actions of supporting the trust's security officers and placing a belief in their ability to make useful contributions completely changed the complexion of criminality across both hospitals.

Staff Accommodation

The isolated nature of our fragmented sites of accommodation raised the issue of vulnerability. This was quickly seized upon by staff – mostly students – who voted with their feet and quickly found more suitable lodgings nearer the city centre. Alternative accommodation was built near Wythenshawe Hospital, but reluctance by staff to move in still prevailed as there were persistent incidents of vandalism and theft in and around this relatively new building. I turned to our local team of PCSOs. Their office was several miles from the hospital, and as we were unable to let all of our available flats they welcomed the offer to rehouse their unit within our accommodation complex. Crime and vandalism suddenly fell out of favour, and staff-accommodation vacancies were reduced to an acceptable level.

These officers were now visual on the hospital site and more frequently seen on patrol in and across Wythenshawe. They regularly attended and contributed to our quarterly security meetings between security officers, PCSOs and local residents, and in the process they forged a positive working relationship and a mutual trust with other managers and our security team. All these actions and efforts culminated in a dramatic reduction in the trust's reported criminal assaults on staff and other crime incidents, consistently painting a picture showing that Wythenshawe Hospital had fewer incidents reported for each 1,000 members of staff than any comparable trust in the north-west of England. It was also reinforcing the same principle, discussed earlier, of policing 'in your street' – but more like 'on your corridor' – to promote social contact and the advantages of proximity. Nevertheless I experienced a lingering undercurrent of intransigence to embrace change. This may exist across many hospital departments, but in my knowledge it was confined locally to the department within which I worked. I will return to this subject and some related issues later in this book.

The Hospital Is on Fire

Just when we thought our hospital security was impregnable this happened. The crux of a phone message I received whilst at home late one summer's evening was that the hospital was on fire. The trust's risk manager had been informed by a member of staff, and he alerted me of this incident.

Many experienced police officers will acknowledge that detecting arson can be most difficult, and as I drove into Wythenshawe I was recounting the number of recent incidents where small fires had been started at different places across the site. Within the previous three months five relatively small fires had been started, resulting in little damage but requiring hospital waste material to be removed by an outside contractor. Could there be any connection? With so many unanswered questions in my mind I called Security Control, obtained an update about the fire from the security supervisor and instructed him not to refer to me in any radio broadcasts. If these fires had been started deliberately, would the perpetrator be at the scene observing his or her handiwork? It wouldn't be the first time that an arsonist had watched and revelled in the effects of their actions.

The wards affected by smoke had been evacuated by staff and our security team, and the effects of the smoke were expected to be temporary. As I threaded my way along passages and alleys, getting nearer and nearer to the scene, smoke density increased, but there was still a visibility range of about twenty yards. I stopped outside the hospital building near the affected wards, stood in the shadows and watched to see if anything unusual could be seen.

A Lurking Suspect

There was nothing out of the ordinary at first. Then still standing in the shadows, I saw someone I recognised. I couldn't believe it. What was he doing here? Who had alerted him? Surely it couldn't be him? I refused to believe what I was looking at. After a few minutes he moved away. I pressed myself against the wall of the building to reduce any risk of being seen and remained motionless in the shadows with a mind full of questions. Nothing made sense.

First of all I needed to investigate the source and cause of the fire. I took another walk around the area, then I broke radio silence. A security officer would guide me to the source of the fire and my investigations had begun.

Hospital waste in a large mobile bin had been set alight near a lift shaft, which had acted as a funnel for the ensuing smoke. Smoke had then flooded into the wards, where elderly patients had settled down for the night and were asleep. It couldn't have been accidental. Someone had devised a plan to cause mayhem by setting small fires, none of which had any life-threatening possibilities until this one. I concluded that all the recent fires and this one were connected and the work of the same person. What was the reason behind them? They caused more inconvenience than anything else, but this latest one had what I was inclined to believe were unintended consequences. Could that have been why the person seen watching the dense smoke swirling around the hospital buildings had visited the hospital – to help if he was needed? That wasn't normally a trait of arsonists, but I had worked near this person. He was highly respected by his peers and I had found him to be one of the better employees of the company he was working for. All this did was to make it more difficult to believe. I wondered if I was suspecting the wrong person.

The chief executive's debrief took place the following morning. I sat for an hour listening to managers in one way or another saying, "It wasn't me, gov!" – which didn't take my enquiries one jot further or surprise me in the least. I gave a brief account of our security officers' actions triggered by their observations from our CCTV cameras. They had obviously acted in a spontaneous manner, all hands assisting the nursing staff on the wards, and no doubt they had reduced a serious situation to a manageable one. The position of the waste transporter under one of our security surveillance cameras wasn't coincidence. Our contractor and I had previously included this in our site inspection when installing CCTV across the hospital site. It had proved its worth and had enabled our security to respond upon seeing the holding area filling with smoke.

Later that same day the chief executive and I walked around the area affected by the smoke damage.

The Chief Executive's Debrief

This chief executive had realised that there was more to this fire than met the eye. In fact there were many issues that needed to be brought to light outside the earlier meeting. Our walkbout lasted for about an hour. The chief executive was brutally frank and I was brutally honest. I had a suspect, but his identity wasn't for common consumption. My evidence was inconclusive. I hadn't seen him do anything. I had no idea of his motive and, perhaps more importantly, I didn't have any other suspects.

At the end of our walkabout the chief executive suddenly turned to me, now almost nose to nose, stared directly into my eyes and said, "What the hell am I going to do now?"

The course of action tentatively agreed upon was that the suspect would be interviewed with the intention of terminating his employment, but the recurring question was what if this is an incorrect decision? As we had suffered six arson attacks we decided that we would only have certain proof if there wasn't any future reoccurrence. In deciding this punitive course of action, the chief executive had shown to me that it wasn't an off-the-cuff decision. It would be taken in an effort to protect the safety of hospital patients and employees.

Many of the forthcoming days were tinged with suspense. We

had a nagging eye on daily nursing supervisors' reports, hoping against hope that no unexplained fires had been reported. Our night security officers were on full alert to spot any questionable piles of rubbish left in unlikely places.

Action Plan

The chief executive and I decided that I would confidentially interview the suspect's general manager prior to the chief executive's intervention. The manager could be relied upon to keep this explosive information under his hat. His reaction wasn't quite what I expected. He found it difficult to restrain himself. It almost became a physical punch-up in his office, but it didn't. It was a bombshell to him. He refused to believe it and made no secret of his feelings, which effectively amounted to him believing I had gone completely mad.

'Anonymous' Letter

Then events took an unexpected turn (Agatha Christie should be writing this). An 'anonymous' letter was received in the post. At first reading, I thought some unbalanced person had written it; but I thought there was something in it, so I read it a couple of times. The writer had given his name and address, but the first line started, 'This is an anonymous letter.' At that point I had a strong feeling that this was not genuine. Further into the letter, the writer gave precise details of a meeting between the manager of a salvage/cleaning company and the suspect, where an envelope containing money would be passed to him. This payment was for using the salvage/cleaning company to clean up and dispose of any rubbish left as a result of the six fires.

I didn't know whether to believe this information or not, but decided I couldn't afford to ignore it. At the appointed time both parties arrived at their agreed location and the envelope containing the payment changed hands. Proof enough, but my feeling was one of overwhelming disappointment. The 'anonymous'-letter writer later revealed he had become involved in a dispute with his boss and felt this would be a way of getting his own back, but he hadn't expected the case to result in our employee's dismissal. It was the end to a sad affair. An excellent employee had weakened in the face of temptation. Furthermore, nothing was made public about the affair and the employee quietly left his employment at the hospital.

That non-disclosure policy was a course of action I had pursued since coming to the trust. The errant employee left his employment in the trust, which maintained the principle that no one can gain by washing the trust's dirty washing in the public domain.

Retreating from Responsibilities

Working in the NHS is probably similar to other occupations in that there is always that ever present feeling that much of life swirls around many desktops. Inevitably that contains good and bad experiences, and most employees rise above these demands. My role may have been slightly different insofar that many police officers and their counterparts in the NHS have an unwritten supportive bond which makes them extremely reluctant to make criticisms of colleagues. Dangers inherent in this unremitting blind camaraderie are not part of my story. Nevertheless a couple of circumstances in particular offended all these principles and convinced me that I should reveal my experiences, hoping against hope that doing so will assist others during their time of need. To set the scene I have given an airing to several incidents that reflect the not-so-professional standards that I experienced.

The scene reminds me of the football managers of either of our two top Manchester teams as they prowl around their limited space adjacent to the playing area. Whilst they have selected their most appropriate players, essentially they are monitoring individual performances to secure the result they desire, which is driven by their need to be accountable to their masters. In the absence of this final tier of supervision, all manner of inconsistencies may develop.

During the early years of the twenty-first century, and shortly after the installation of the electric fence around the staff car park at Wythenshawe Hospital, it was found that improvements were required to the parking surface. Many staff were avoiding large areas with unsuitable parking surfaces.

Contractors moved in and began carrying out their improvements. They removed the top layer of soil, exposing solid clay, and started to cover it with a thin layer of shale. I had a discussion with the contractor and NHS Estates staff about my concerns around this drainage issue, but to no avail.

Heavy rain sometime later caused some tremendous problems. Large areas of the car park were quickly transformed into a duck pond, effectively stranding parked cars. Two pairs of wellington boots were purchased to enable our security officers to retrieve the forlorn cars. The sight of staff (mainly female) stood around a lake was extremely frustrating, but they appreciated the efforts of our security officers.

The following weekend, and for several other weekends, staff (not those responsible for this debacle) volunteered to operate a mechanical digger to establish a land-water drain along the boundary and level a mound of shale hurriedly delivered to provide a buffer between the clay and the top surface. It was totally successful. One of our renowned and most active volunteers was our consultant paediatrician Richard Sawyer, who was also (amongst a myriad other projects he carried out) the trust's environmental ambassador. He planted a couple of dozen trees on and adjacent to this car park.

The main concern was that although our struggles in the floodwaters had been made known to senior managers no support was ever forthcoming. Initially the presence of these 'spittlebugs' in management were largely undetected, but they would re-emerge later with fatal consequences. I have given these villains this identity for two reasons. Firstly some references by staff would be inappropriate to print, and secondly I initially became aware of the presence of spittlebugs when my brothers and sisters and I explored the countryside around Stanthorne. We discovered them on the stems of young wild plants/weeds, and cuckoo spit seemed an apt name for the white froth they produce. The life cycle of the bugs on the host plant mimics the behaviour of our migrant selfish bird – the cuckoo.

In more recent times (2014) the visitor-car-park controls

were updated, which immediately caused uproar amongst the uniformed security staff. Visitor-car-park pay stations were replaced, which was the reason the security supervisor was stood outside my office as I arrived for work one morning. He was clearly agitated about the replacement of our previously installed secure cash safe-box system for collecting car-park fees, and he wasn't going to be placated until I accompanied him to examine these new installations. I arranged for the senior manager (Spittlebug 1), who had the responsibility for these installations, to accompany us on this inspection tour. The system was totally unsafe for our security officers to operate insofar that an open bucket-type receptacle had replaced the secure safe box. There was now in place a level of temptation for staff to interfere with staff-car-parking income previously unknown at this trust. It was breathtakingly naïve, but the trap had been set.

Not satisfied with this level of response, I consulted the engineer tasked with overseeing the installations. He protested that he had delivered a scheme within the budget allowed, and furthermore Spitalbug 2 had signed it off. It would have been more successful to have given ice cream in cones to half a dozen children with instructions not to eat them whilst you left them unsupervised. This senior manager assuaged the objections from the security supervisor by promising to take his concerns to the relevant manager.

This plot to ensnare our security officers had been uncovered, but three weeks later, after no action had been taken, the security supervisor left his employment at Wythenshawe Hospital. The incompetence around this new scheme had simply created dangerous and unsafe working conditions. It was obvious that the creation of this system had been created intentionally or by totally incompetent staff, but it wasn't at all clear why the safety of staff had been so blatantly overlooked.

As several members of staff were likely to be called upon to assist with minor fault rectifications, I immediately arranged a meeting with them. In essence, and without mincing words, they were prewarned that this was a cynical trap and under no circumstances were they to attend unaccompanied at any of these installations. Twelve months after I had retired from the trust half a dozen security staff would weaken in their resolve and receive custodial sentences. The real villains (Spittlebugs 1, 2 and 3) have much to answer for.

The case concerning the trust's car-park manager was another particularly sad and damning episode. The same three villains (Spittlebugs 1, 2 and 3) would be fully implicated. The car-park manager had been in his post for about ten years and had faithfully carried out his duties, which required him to meet every new member of staff and provide them with a photographic identification card which incorporated access to our electronic doors and car-park barrier systems. He also maintained the trust's contacts with residents local to the hospital and our resident PCSOs, bringing them together on a quarterly basis to discuss security, safety and car-parking issues.

It was at one of these quarterly meetings that we witnessed behaviour by another senior manager that would shock all present – a sudden explosion of temper and verbal threats, disrespect to our guests and his immediate departure from the meeting. Our car-park manager was visibly upset by this action, and ten minutes after I had closed the meeting he presented a written statement of complaint against this manager. The car-park manager and I later agreed not to pursue it. But this senior manager now had another vendetta to pursue.

Our car-park manager, whilst immensely efficient, was under great pressure to keep on top of his work. Many of his parking queries submitted by staff were rerouted to me and I utilised a member of the trust's security team to give part-time assistance to him. Twelve months later the senior manager (Spitalbug 2) directed that this person should be removed from his position. No explanation was given, and when asked still none was given.

I made a written complaint to the chief executive, setting out the nature of the existing oppressive, dictatorial, threatening and inconsiderate management style. It concluded with the chief executive making his obvious displeasure known about the events leading to the hearing, and I felt his decision gave me some justification for raising the lid on the antics staff had experienced. Then it all fell apart. He concluded the hearing by making an offer of monetary compensation if I signed a non-disclosure agreement. He hadn't listened. He hadn't researched my personal pedigree. Sweeping issues of this nature under the carpet is why the NHS is in some kind of terminal decline. I declined both offers.

Some months later our car-park manager experienced a domestic upheaval which required him to leave his existing marital accommodation. This ignited an unforeseen health problem. He became homeless and after several rescue attempts, which required me to drag him from the gutter and get him temporarily rehoused in the trust's staff accommodation, he finally made a return to work and resumed his previous role. The main driver for this was an association he had formed with a young married mother, which appeared to be successful ultimately culminating in his cohabiting with her family. He experienced one relapse, obtaining the statutory sick note to cover a week's absence. This breached his annual allocation of sick leave by a couple of days.

Two of our senior managers (Spitalbugs 1 and 2) held a disciplinary hearing, prior to which I visited one of them to inform him that it was important to our car-park manager's well-being that he should retain his position at the trust. Not allowing him to do so would effectively equate to passing a death sentence on him. I didn't mince my words.

Their response was a reply that wasn't expected and left nothing to discuss: "That is not within my job description."

No witnesses were called to this hearing, and despite my earlier protestations his services were dispensed with. He totally fell apart and passed away eighteen months later. I had earlier recognised that he had become seriously mentally ill, which he had concealed most effectively, but these two senior managers (Spittlebugs 1 and 2) were not about to muddy their own personal waters and in the absence of any accountability they abandoned one of their own loyal servants.

Another reprehensible practice would find an employee hiding within the well of the desk to escape from Spittlebugs 2's attention as he walked through the office. This initial revelation was difficult to believe as it seemed more appropriate in a television comedy script, but the reasons which drove these actions give an insight into the hatred and despair caused by an existing management system which was devoid of accountability.

This period of management by Wythenshawe's three 'spittle bugs' was set to run out of their life cycle. This was precipitated by a phone call I received requesting my attendance with a consultant manager, who on the face of it was scrutinising our current management systems. Why would anyone bother to ask me? What could be the real agenda? The interviewer was a former NHS chief executive.

We used the director's office and sat opposite each other across a large desk. He had chosen a day to visit when the director wasn't around. I wondered if that could be a clue. Initially we didn't speak. Could he be playing some kind of cat-and-mouse game, I wondered. If so, my mind was on full alert. I decided that he would need to make the first move. He shuffled several papers which he carried into the office with him. My gaze was firmly on him.

I leant back in my chair and remember thinking, 'After you.'

Slowly he stopped shuffling his papers, looked up at me and asked three questions. He wanted my opinion about the three Wythenshawe 'spittlebugs'.

I hesitantly leant forward, and as I did so I thought of my colleagues who still had what to them might seem like a lifetime to work with this oppressive management. I decided I owed it to them to describe them as they deserved, including warts and all.

He quickly got to discussing many management issues which required him to visit me again. This he did, and both interviews concluded most amicably.

A couple of months later Spittlebug 1 was last seen leaving the trust in a cloudy haze of inner conversations with unknown persons, oblivious to his immediate surroundings and walking quickly to the car-park exit. Spittlebugs 2 and 3 retired a couple of months later.

To be fair, I didn't reveal that I suspected our car-park manager was struggling with some serious mental-health issues. It was the first time I had encountered these health conditions, but at least I had realised what I don't think is universally recognised about this condition: that work colleagues make every effort to disguise their weakness. They don't knock on your door and say they feel as if they are turning into a fruit cake. It just doesn't happen like that in real life. Any challenges over these issues are almost certainly met with denial, and convincing ones at that. The irony is that he was one of the most popular employees at a large NHS hospital; he was seriously ill and yet help when needed wasn't there. How could he have slipped off the radar of our senior management in an organisation that has health experts in every other office?

The experience took my mind back to an earlier staff-training session I was delivering at which several senior nurses were present. During some ensuing conversations it was revealed that two of these nurses had joined the trust some thirty years earlier and were actually working in neighbouring wards, yet this meeting was the first time they had met since they joined the trust what seemed to them to be a lifetime ago. They had used the same staff car park and entered the hospital through the same door. Although their shift patterns had a small part to play in their lack of personal contact, nevertheless it remains difficult to grasp, when human social interaction is becoming more important than ever, that close proximity still requires an element of human effort to communicate in the face of intense working pressures and needs to be the driver in management practices. Nevertheless in 2019 Manchester NHS Foundation Trust is actively pursuing a policy of encouraging staff to speak out, to allow management to nip problems in the bud.

Cycling for Health

In 2007 a local GP (Harry Lowe) approached me with his idea of forming a cycling club for the trust's staff. This would have been during one of the trust's open days, but at first I wasn't quite bowled over with the idea. However, other people on the security stand had greater interests in cycling and general travel planning, and we decided to give it a go. Staff donated scores of old bikes and a local resident stepped forward and devoted his time and expertise to making them roadworthy. Barbara taught young children to ride as well as overseas student nurses who joined in our rides.

An important issue emanating from this initial discussion was that my hitherto seven-day working week was coming to an end, and to break this practice we gathered several cyclists to form our club and accompany Harry. Without realising it, this would be a life-changing event.

In 2018 we celebrated our tenth year as a club, taking part in and supporting the Annual Christie 100K Cycling Fundraising Event in aid of beating cancer. The club meet weekly (Saturdays and Sundays) and basically get absorbed in their excursions into the Cheshire countryside whilst fulfilling their quota of health-promoting personal exercise.

A by-product of their cycling is their increased knowledge of countryside matters, which by far exceeds their early cycling days when if it had a beak, wings and flew it was a bird. During appropriate seasons eyes search the skies for the arrival of swifts and swallows, which we see as harbingers of warmer weather, and usually a rider will direct our attention to lapwings (peewits), which tumble around in the sky to attract us away from their young. As ground-nesting birds they are vulnerable until fully fledged. Skylarks have much in common with lapwings, but their hovering at height emitting a constant and unvarying song hasn't been heard for several years. We feel this may be due to our rides taking place during the afternoon.

Team Leader

Our unsung inspirational hero is our volunteer team leader Brian Sherwood. He is only too happy to go that extra mile for anyone. On the Sunday rides he uses his own tandem and has a blind person riding pillion. The following is just one example of his many 'knight of the road' good deeds.

It was on one of the Saturday rides that he observed a leather wallet lying on the roadside grass verge. I examined it for him, noted the amount of money and important documents and concluded that there were sufficient identity documents for him to pay a visit to the believed owner. The next day with the blind rider behind him they carried out the visit. I'll let his explanation tell the story.

"We rode into this cul-de-sac and approached this posh house in Wilmslow. I didn't feel happy about it at all. I didn't think we were allowed into this cul-de-sac because all the houses must be worth millions of pounds each. Anyway, I knocked on the front door. No one answered, but a chap in the next-door garden came to us offering his help. I gave him the wallet. He phoned his neighbour and I think you could say he was overcome with relief."

The following week Brian received a thank-you letter and sufficient cash to purchase two of their favourite 'big breakfast' meals.

A Blind Cyclist and a Bow-and-Arrow Licence

On another occasion our team leader curtailed the intended route in the face of some inclement weather which appeared to be closing in on us, and we called at a small country pub in Mobberley. We all parked our bikes and made our way to the fireside, where we would all enjoy tea and toast. We joined two other males, who turned out to be father and son. I was the first to join these two, but was closely followed by Barbara and our blind pillion rider. Brian was securing the bikes. This father and son could clearly see from our outer garments that we were from the Wythenshawe Hospital Cycling Club. The younger of the two had his interest aroused by the sight of our blind cyclist, wearing his black-lens goggles, and started to enquire about his mode of transport. Unfortunately for him, a recent television programme had included research into the habits of bats and their unique ability to navigate in the dark. The plot was set. We all sat around the fireside whilst Barbara explained that our blind cyclist, Peter Royle, was also assisting in this research and was equipped with special *Tomorrow's World* gismos, which he was trying out under the supervision of our cycling team.

They placed their pints of beer back on the table, and after several attempts managed to get two coherent sentences together. By now all the team had gathered around the fire. No one flinched. Half a dozen faces with serious expressions peered at the two drinkers. They appeared to visibly lose interest in their beer and soaked up this make-believe story of our blind rider. To add to the authenticity of the tale, Peter had received his refreshments and had his hands guided to the cups and plates. They totally believed Peter could ride his bike along country lanes and in traffic although he was totally blind.

Barbara couldn't keep up the pretence any more and spilled the beans. Everyone shared in the tale with great humour. But then came the twist: the younger of the two drinkers revealed that he had served for thirty years in the Cheshire Constabulary and at Wilmslow. His only distinction was that he was the only police officer in the country to ever issue a bow-and-arrow licence. He insisted on telling his story and that, unlike our story, was a true-life incident.

A father and his young son called at Wilmslow Police Station, where the storyteller was the office constable. The father was at his wits' end as his son repeatedly shot his arrow at the neighbours' animals despite threats to destroy the bow if he persisted. The Constable was his last hope. Upon hearing the father's plight he arranged for the father and son to visit Wilmslow Police Station each Saturday morning for the next four weeks. He would escort them into the rear yard of the police station and set up some form of target practice. So far so good. The boy became most proficient and left on the fourth Saturday with a delighted father – the son had given him his solemn promise only to shoot the arrows at the target his father had placed in the rear garden, whereupon the Constable had issued a bow-and-arrow licence to the father. He was now the best friend of both the father and the son. The father wished to bring the Constable's actions to the notice of the Chief Constable and wrote to him. To issue the licence the Constable had used an official form, and it was this which amounted to his undoing. He was summoned to headquarters at Chester and the result of his disciplinary charge (inappropriate use of constabulary stationery) was that he would perform office duties at Wilmslow for the remainder of his service. But with great pride he told us that this was his claim to fame as he remained the only police officer in England ever to issue a bow-and-arrow licence.

Another worthy involvement was that of two female nurses from Northern Europe who were seconded to the trust on a twelve-month basis. Brian Sherwood created two roadworthy bikes and loaned them to these two ladies, who seemed to become permanently attached to them as they cycled everywhere in addition to joining our Saturday cycling teams. A couple of days before returning home I received a thank-you postcard. The lump-in-the-throat moment came towards the end of their note as they closed with the words 'Cycling with the team gave us both the most enjoyable times we had whilst at Wythenshawe Hospital.'

To further encourage staff to become involved, I created and distributed a 'Cycling Summary' a few days after each ride. They were eagerly read by many staff, who often made comments about their enjoyment in accompanying us on the rides, if only in spirit. I hope that small seed of interest may manifest into a lasting involvement – if not for them, maybe for their families and friends – together with my best wishes of always having fair weather and gentle breezes.

Volunteering

This is a most important arm of hospital services, and the small number of active members have always appeared to me to be doing a great job. Since retiring from the police I served for ten years as chair of the Manchester South Scouts and spent many hours fundraising for various good causes, including organising and attending car-boot events, selling various fundraising items – in those early days we even included plants and flowers supplied by a local grower. As the majority of these events were held on hospital premises, our on-site security officers were an integral part of these activities. I concluded these efforts after delivering a cheque for the amount of £40,000 to support the MRI scanner appeal.

Latterly I gave two very interesting years as a hospital governor.

One day I received a letter via the post office that I didn't open until later that day. I need to explain that it referred to my actions when I gave evidence at Manchester Crown Court as a witness to support my old colleague the Scoutmaster Ron Hey (see Chapter 12). It simply read, 'When I needed a friend you were there'.

Currently Barbara and I still support the trust's cycling club and ride most Saturdays. I feel there are many of the trust's employees (about eighty per cent are female) who live within five miles of the hospital and just can't make that all-important and life-saving step of getting on a bike.

These lifetime recollections are about belief. Our team are committed to having belief in you, and our team leader continually demonstrates this belief as he rides at the pace of the slowest rider.

Also, for those who are 'never-ridden-a-bike-before' cyclists, we have routes through our local parks (Wythenshawe/Sale Water Parks).

I will let our blind rider, now retired (Peter Royle), do the talking. When cycling in the team with him he appreciates nothing more than for me or the team leader to give him a running commentary about the countryside we are cycling through. In my case this can go on for probably ten minutes or so until I next come forward out of the group to give him another update. Throughout the time that my commentary continues his face, partially covered by his black-lens goggles, lights up with a semi-permanent smile, betraying the obvious delight he derives from cycling. If you share the same feeling as myself, you would find this a most humbling experience, but when I asked what he would do if he ever regained his sight his spontaneous reply was, "I would buy myself a new bike and ride every day with Brian." No other answer was required; none was given.

So for those waverers who are waiting for that inevitable NHS walking stick before they get the message, speak to the volunteering section and they will pass you on to Brian.

CHAPTER 15

CONCLUSIONS

My journey began during the Second World War and recalled my family circumstances during those dangerous and trying times. I described our living conditions and the struggles as I saw them, particularly as I watched my mother wrestling with the demands of five children, food, clothing, coal rationing and the severe cold weather, which seemed a co-conspirator to make life even harder than it should have been. As if that wasn't enough, to test her resolve my father died amidst this turmoil, leaving the added demand of seeking out ways to raise sufficient income to maintain the family group. She made many sacrifices, some of which I am sure she shielded from her children, but against all these odds she succeeded. She was a forthright and no-nonsense mother, but she was imbued with one other enduring quality (about which she would never brook any weakening of her resolve): she always remained a very humble person and strove to ingrain that characteristic in all her children. And she always reminded us that humility costs nothing. Later in her life her now six children, some of whom settled with their families as far away as Canada, would unconsciously portray and demonstrate this quality which binds them all together.

I have tried to bring some life back into many distant and fading memories, and I accept that in doing so I will have omitted some important and interesting issues, but hope I have recalled the most important ones. Also I know I will have forgotten to mention some everyday yet influential people, but this only goes to illustrate my own frailties, and I offer my sincere apologies. The course of my journey is littered with collisions; some encounters were brief, with many people like you, some arising out of unlikely situations, and many were with people who were in their own way influential. The general common denominator among the influential people is that they all exuded varying degrees of belief in me and others around them. This belief is inclusive – you will always have a part to play.

Playing football in the street triggered my first encounter with a most influential person who just happened to be our milkman. I explained how he made time in his busy life to help that schoolboy who couldn't add together two and two for love nor money.

This is my life story, and unavoidably it includes commentary on bygone days. To ensure it retains a link with reality I have made several references to people I found less than inspiring. That's life. The purpose is to reveal life's uncertainties. It isn't necessary to identify culprits as the issues explained can easily be identified and I am sure are as prevalent today in some form or other as they ever were. I only point out shortcomings which I witnessed or had experience of. Some of these issues brought back memories of a management incident during my early policing days. The staff-appraisal system was such that infrequently a probationary constable would find it difficult to deliver the service irrespective of the best efforts of their colleagues and sergeants. In one case a commander presented the case of a failing officer to the Chief Constable and was unexpectedly given the 'bums rush' with the message that the officer was failing because his supervision was not up to the task. At the time this was a ground-breaking message. This culminated in the failing officer undergoing a period of retraining using the close support of his colleagues. It worked.

My two years spent walking the streets of Stalybridge revealed a policing system that allowed the existence of a Second World War prisoner-of-war-camp mentality because of the lack of interactive supervision from the higher echelons of the service, which left an indelible scar by effectively having my name stolen and replacing it by a number. Their lack of accountability has been mentioned elsewhere. It was always a relief to escape from the parading on and off routine, to walk into that town with 'those cobbled streets and warm-hearted folk who, without realising it first instilled in me the moral values and aspirations which have ever since guided and sustained me' (Eli Hague).

Further criticisms of the police service were given as we hastened the creation of police suburban wastelands, effectively becoming largely anonymous amongst those people we call our communities and inadvertently cutting off our essential lifeblood. That point was made out of the blue by the person I named Miss Marple during my early days at Wythenshawe, and her remarks led to a proactive policing strategy that changed the face of policing by creating Parish Policing and placed police officers in all the places used by residents and their families. It wasn't plain sailing and I was even threatened with arrest by a resident at her front door. (There's an imposter on my doorstep!) The sergeant's response was straight off the top shelf of police humour and one which I always recollect with a smile.

As a traffic cop I used two instances of personal involvement in delivering close-proximity training, the recipients of which developed successful police and clergy careers. The first relied more on instinct, life's experiences and personal confidence mixed with a large dose of luck (the robbery of a taxi driver), and the second accompanied by that ever present police humour (fish and chips and two prisoners). Both incidents portray a two-way personal trust and belief – the main themes resonating throughout my story.

My early years in agriculture left me with an indelible scar which surfaces with references to that shoulder-to-shoulder existence with nature. For example, gardeners know that throwing seed on to barren and infertile soil is a wasted exercise; similarly reinventing social contacts and general communications is like working in a garden, replacing fading plants and seeing the timely rejuvenating effects of pruning on shrubs and trees. The pruning effect within our social contacts is much the same. Essentially the presence of a life cycle controlling most things within our existence is something to be continually aware of. Humans need to know they belong as we seem wired for frequent and genuine social interactions. This probably reflects positively about our policing success at Wythenshawe, which was rooted in the regeneration of social contacts between neighbours. As a result, everything spread outwards like that newly pruned tree.

Time, however, doesn't stand still, and it hardly seems like a week passes by without some revelation of shortcomings or failures in the police and NHS. These are early warnings – unless some attention is given they will inevitably mimic those maturing blooms in the garden that run to seed. I hope others unfortunate enough to experience enclaves infested with the equivalent of that spittlebug on otherwise effective and efficient staff may feel justified in challenging established practices where they feel there is some justification, and possibly influence changes to effect improvements.

My earliest experiences in life shaped my lifelong views. A close family unit, eating meals, playing games and arguing around the kitchen table, together with supportive neighbours and excellent school teachers at Middlewich High School, provided the springboard into life that today in the twenty-first century young people in this digital age can only dream of. The demise of local corner shops should be resisted at all costs. The village cinema is now long gone, where I stood in a long queue tightly grasping my sister's hand, tingling with excitement, waiting with other village folk to see our first film. Feature films, such as *Black Beauty* and *Gone with the Wind*, were supported by cowboy films in which Roy Rogers or Gene Autry starred. These community hubs have largely been replaced by twenty-first-century leisure pursuits which require the support of us all, irrespective of age, etc.

My own community service started in the police service. It embraced the Scout Association, and the Scoutmaster example of the sort of unsung hero who could be living in a street near you.

Throwing in the towel in the face of large supermarkets is a concern our councillors need to treat as an 'over my dead body' type of challenge, but it is a challenge which also represents opportunities. In an era where market forces dictate, unless they carry their communities with them they are likely to succumb to the forces of competition.

Frequent revelations of shortcomings in public-service companies reflect a stark absence of accountability. This includes the constabulary. They would do well to refocus their efforts to create social contacts and reinforce mutual respect amongst our communities – in other words, return to creating meaningful contacts. Time spent pursuing these investments will reap unexpected rewards. I used the example encountered at one stage in my police career when I was faced with the dilemma of closing a police station, thereby cutting off public access to their police. The importance of that welcoming beacon shining out brightly to our 'customers' on a dark, cold night of rainswept streets cannot be underestimated. The necessity to pursue face-to-face contacts is evident throughout; the importance becomes reality when absence of authority leads to withdrawal from the streets, quickly to be replaced by undesirable elements and antisocial behaviour, including the serious violence and drug use currently plaguing our conurbations. My experience at Fairywell convinced me of the merits of utilising suitable candidates to pursue community projects as an alternative to custodial sentences.

Similarly the lack of accountability in our public services is evident to all, and fresh examples emerge on almost a weekly basis.

A couple of hundred years ago Edmund Burke is reported to have made the comment that 'To allow evil to flourish it is only necessary for good men to do nothing.' That seems as relevant today as ever it was.

Ultimately I thrived at school along with my brothers and sisters as we were sustained by a caring mother, and later I was also helped by several inspirational employers and friends. I failed my eleven-plus exam, but hopefully I succeeded in convincing others that life reflects that garden border as a continuing process, culminating in my case in many achievements which are explained elsewhere in my story. It simply reflects the importance of accepting the presence of a life cycle in everything we do. Many of life's achievements can be achieved later in life and only you can plough your life's furrow.

Finally, I was fortunate to have sight of a book *The Village Effect* written by a Canadian psychologist, Susan Pinker, who uses the field of neuroscience and her own experiences and research to explain why face-to-face contact is now more important than it ever was – social contact is a biological drive that online communication just doesn't quite get. She maintains amongst other things that we need to prioritise our social interactions and that face-to-face contact at home, school and work makes us healthier, smarter and more successful. She also argues that time spent with neighbours will enrich and extend your life. Frequent human contact is at least as important to our survival as clean air or good nutrition. You may be persuaded to agree, but whichever side you settle on there is no class distinction or price tag – something which my mother also preached to all her children a lifetime ago.

The title of my book simply identifies the importance of belief and mutual trust, which can so easily get lost in this age driven by work, school and home practices that perpetuate minimal human contact and activities.